Mind Field

The Keys To Mastering Accomplishment
Make Things Right! Control Your Destiny! Master Your World!

Milton Howard, Jr.

Mind Field

Copyright © 2012 by Milton Howard, Jr.

All rights reserved. No part of this book may be reproduced or transmitted in any form or by any means without written permission of the author.

ISBN 978-1480164079

Table of Contents

The Psychology of the Mind Field   1
Setting the Energy for an Extraordinary Life

The Hauntings of the Mind Field   9
What Stops You When You Want More

The Callings of the Mind Field   17
Tuning Your Life for More Success

The Four Components of the Mind Field   37
Relationships that Lead to Results

The Time and Timing of the Mind Field   53
Getting What You Want When You Want

The Music of the Mind Field   69
The Making of a Genius

The Science of the Mind Field   81
When Success Becomes Law

The Spirit of the Mind Field   93
From Small to Big

Appendix   109

The Psychology of the Mind Field

Accomplishment is at the core of every human spirit. With this being the case, accomplishment can also seem allusive at times. There are some who seem to have the Midas touch when it comes to accomplishment, and everything that they touch turns to gold. Accomplishment for them seems to be effortless. For others, accomplishment on a regular basis is just not there. What is the difference? Not being able to get what you want when you want can be frustrating at times. Surely after putting a lot of time and effort into something and then not have it not turn out the way you like it can be annoying.

Mind Field is designed to get you on the road to accomplishment, to make accomplishment a regular occurrence in your life, and then most of all, Mind Field will give you the confidence of accomplishment before you start on what you want to achieve. Achieving what you want in life will become a norm as you get a grasp on the Mind Field and the power that it has to drive you towards having the things you want and the life you want. For those who fair well on the side of accomplishment, get ready to accelerate your efforts. Let's get started by exploring the Mind Field.

The Mind Field is the arrangement of the people, places, and things around you. It is with the people, places, and the things around you that you are in a constant state of exchange. This exchange bubbles up and creates an energy field or a system of energy that is parlayed into a highway of thought patterns. Your thoughts are not who you are because your thoughts are a separate entity that travels within this energy field. This is an energy field resulting from the exchanges that you make.

Energy is a privilege to know, but a responsibility to transform. Yes, we are all charged with the task to be successful.

What we must do is increase our intelligence of what exists outside of ourselves and inside as it concerns energy. Most call the outside realm of energy the spiritual realm, and some simply call it the unseen realm. Whatever you may call it, it is all forms of energy. I call it the Mind Field. This is my attempt to give this unseen or spiritual realm a comprehensive breakdown so more people can understand it and use it for their highest benefit. For most of us, what is unseen is broken down into digestible bits of understanding, which is sometimes regulated by Western religious ideology or the field of psychology. It is widely understood that our thoughts and our thinking are the product of the mind.

For now, here's a statement you have to accept by faith. Thoughts exist outside of your ability to think them. Thoughts here are a matter of tuning. Tuning into what? You tune into thoughts. What thoughts? Thoughts that exist outside of you: one, for observation of those same thoughts, and secondly to build relationships to those very thoughts. Whatever your life is tuned into, it will determine the level, type, quantity, and quality of the thoughts received by you. This again, in turn determines your quality of living. That's why when your thinking is off and seems to be uncontrollable, or out-of-control, you can take some medications and tune into a whole different batch of thoughts. Since medication can affect what you tune into, it proves that all thoughts are separate from who you actually are.

Life is about tuning, and tuning is about the arrangements that are made in your life. The only real struggle in life is the struggle of tuning; the people that we tune into, the places that we tune into, the things that we tune into, and then the tunes that we send out from our own being. This struggle stems from being ignorant of the fact that you hold this power - the power of tuning.

The only struggle in life is a struggle of tuning.

You have the power to tune simply because you have the power of arrangements in your life and your thoughts can thusly be arranged and controlled.

Let me give you some proofs...

Have you ever awakened in the morning, listless and everything seems negative, and you really couldn't tell what was wrong, but the day just wasn't right? But nothing happened the previous day to justify that feeling.

Have you ever been at a party where the party was going well and somebody walked in that was a known party pooper, and your consciousness of how the day would go immediately changed?

Have you been to the movies and you just knew something bad was going to happen in the next scene because the music turned dark and scary?

These are just some examples of how your thought process is tuned and can be retuned immediately as circumstances and the environment changes around you.

Tuning – The Main Feature of the Mind Field

When it comes to the Mind Field, I want you to first consider two types of tuning:

ET - Electronic Tuning   **MT - Musical Tuning**

Electronic tuning works much like a TV or a radio. You tune in by switching channels. Musical tuning is just what it is. It is adjusting the tone or the sound of an instrument to match other instruments that are playing with you. It is also a sound or a tone that you put out. Using both examples, I will show you that the mind works in much the same way. In order to be more successful in life, you can tune into thought patterns that reflect the success that you are looking for. Like a radio or TV, you simply have to turn the channel of your mind to line up with the frequency of what you want in life.

As far as the musical example is concerned, unlike the TV and radio where you simply change channels to determine what you want in life; with musical tuning, you put out a sound or a tone to align with the matching sounds of life to create a pleasurable existence. The tone or tune that emanates from you will give others the opportunity to tune into the direction that you set so that others can play the vital role of harmonizing with you.

Again, the two types of tuning:

ET - Electronic Tuning   **MT - Musical Tuning**

How We Currently Understand Things

As I said earlier, primarily, the mind is currently understood from two modes of knowledge, specifically Western religious ideology, and then the field of psychological study. Part of Western ideology comes from the standpoint of using spiritual notions to describe the unseen, the mind, and how the mind works in terms of using it to live a successful or at least a comfortable life. Then psychological institutions refer to mental strategies, mental health, and other mentally based ideologies to achieve primarily the same goals.

The mind business is the biggest and most lucrative business in world history. It includes the two primary modes of the mind business; religion and the spiritual, and then the psychological. It also includes the entire educational system, the personal development industry, motivational industry, and much more. Without a healthy mind, it becomes quite difficult to navigate life, and moreover it becomes difficult to live a very successful life. A great deal of money is spent on mastering the mind and getting the mind right. Even when it comes to the spiritual part of it, people by faith will give top dollar to their respective religious institutions with the hope that they will receive helpful information from their spiritual masters and appointed leaders, whether it be pastors, bishops, popes, master teachers, rabbis, and the like. They hope that financing their respective religious institutions would lead to a greater life experience. Bottom line, it all costs, and people are willing to pay big dollars to get their mind right.

**Without a balanced mind,
it becomes impossible to live a balanced life.**

What I would like to do here is give you the structures of the mind that are unique as far as an approach is concerned. My attempt is not to challenge the psychological standards that have been set by industry professionals, or the spiritual standards set by our religious institutions. My attempt here is to give you a unique roadmap of the mind that can be easily understood and readily applied. This is done so that you can get on to the task of living an astounding and incredible life where you meet all your desired goals.

Once you understand the mind structures in this book, you will simply become proficient at tuning. Mind tuning allows you to cut across the vast amount of information available about the mind and strategies used for the mind for life advancement. This is a simple and comprehensive way to master life and to access the more immediate results that you might be looking for.

The Terminology

I want to start by giving you some terms to put into your psychological toolbox that will make this process very easy to understand. These terms become extremely important, because I want to save you time and money when it comes to accessing the life you want and moving to higher levels from where you are. Here are the terms:

Energy Dynamics

Energy dynamics are the pockets of energy surrounding you in an arranged order. This arranged order either enhances your life or it becomes a major draw on your life. You have the power to fully control these dynamics and not leave the energy surrounding you exposed to other energy dynamics and systems that might lead you in undesired directions.

Authentication

Authentication is the process of moving to the next level using the power of others who have your best interest at heart. It takes great relationships to do great things, and it also takes others that have accomplished things before you to authenticate your direction.

Tuning

Tuning is the process of adjusting your mental space to receive thoughts that are more congruent to the direction you would like to head in. Tuning also involves the energy you send out which causes other factors outside of you to tune into your direction that will enhance the likelihood of accomplishment.

Cycles & Seasons

This is the timing and times that are set to bring the desired results into your life. These cycles and seasons are guaranteed, but not always recognized. Higher cycles and seasons that are unrecognized will leave you exposed to lower ones.

Pushing Time

This is the concept of taking your dreams, your goals, and your destiny and tying it into seasons and cycles that are initiated by the relationships that you build. You also use the process of authentication to power yourself towards accomplishment at greater speeds.

Hauntings & Callings

These are the places and spaces in the Mind Field that affect your movements on earth.

Imaging - I mage

The process of setting into the Mind Field the desired results in which you are looking for, so it can be replicated into the physical.

Regeneration

Taking what is replicated from an image in the Mind Field and setting it to regenerate exponentially based on the relationships built. There are only two types of regeneration - repetitive regeneration and exponential regeneration. Repetitive regeneration is when you repeat what you don't like, and exponential regeneration is when you grow to the next level.

Places & Spaces

Components within the Mind Field that we mentally build or recognize that become the image that is reflected into the physical.

House Chambers

A description of the places and spaces in the Mind Field, because these places and spaces become our mental homes. These homes are so real that to understand them in any other way can blind you to the reality that the unseen is always responsible for what can be seen. Giving the places and spaces within the Mind Field the title "House Chambers", denotes the fact that the House Chambers are constructions, therefore they are completely controllable.

The Law of Supply

The law of supply is the understanding that everything that you want in life exist in its entirety already. Therefore, the need to attract things to you is not necessary, but the need to awake to all of your provisions is paramount. This also forms the basis for what I call, "looking for the evidence".

Looking for the Evidence

Instead of accepting what is happening in front of you, you stop and look for the evidence of any and everything that is consistent with your dreams and destiny.

Exponential Growth

Exponential growth is a mindset of how you grow. An exponent of a number is how many times that number is multiplied by itself. Exponential growth is taking your initial successes and repeating the same thing at greater levels.

If you can familiarize yourself with these terms, it will greatly assist you in gaining a new understanding of how the mind works and how easy it is to navigate and construct the mind to advance whatever your heart is set to accomplish.

The Hauntings of the Mind Field

Now let's get into the structures of the Mind Field. I want to start here by describing what I call the hauntings. The hauntings are the initial component of the Mind Field that most people struggle with. The hauntings are events in life that reappear in life as an extreme inconvenience to your ability to move forward. A haunting is a negative event or perception that does just that, it comes back to haunt you, and its presence can paralyze or diminish your decision-making ability. What I want to do here is to give you an example of a haunting that would help you with the definition.

I was traveling to choir rehearsal one day and decided to take a nice scenic route to the church. As I turned on this back road, I made the turn with a clear conscience and with no psychological issues whatsoever with reaching my destination. All of a sudden, I heard this loud pop and the truck I was driving began to shake violently, and so I slowed down. Being an astute driver, I quickly realized that I was dealing with a flat tire. Having the tools necessary to repair the tire gave me great comfort in my ability to make a quick tire change and keep going. It was not so. The object that punched my tire was ominous, and it put a hole in my tire that was larger than normal which rendered the tire beyond repair.

Needless to say, I was unable to make it to rehearsal that day because what should've taken no longer than 7 to 10 minutes, turned into an entire afternoon. I was devastated. But I eventually, with the help of others fixed the tire and headed back home. Now, on my next trip to choir rehearsal, I went the normal route. Even though the new route that I had tried earlier offered me a shorter trip to choir rehearsal and a much more scenic route, something in my mind kept me from going that way again. I called this thought or this something within my mind, a haunting. The shortcut and the scenic route offered greater benefits to getting to my destination, but yet, I stayed off that road.

There was nothing wrong with the road. There was nothing wrong with the new direction, but there was a thought created that kept me off that road. I really began to feel stupid. I was actually deciding time and time again not to drive down that road, but I was listening to a haunting created by the relationship I decided to have with the unfortunate event of having a flat tire on that road. A thought would introduce itself to me each time I left the house saying, "If you go down that road again, you will have a flat tire again". Where did that thought come from? It is this very type of thought that I call a haunting.

I decided one day, what's the likelihood of me having another flat on the same road? This time out, I took the new direction; the short and the scenic route. As I turned down that road, my body began to feel different and my expectations were molded in place by the previous event on that same road. I thought to myself, "this is crazy, why am I feeling this way?" The haunting had become even more magnified, which now affected my behavior as I drove the length of the road. I was looking for big pieces of metal in the street as I drove. This made for a very uncomfortable drive. The haunting had affected the very truth of the matter. I had used this haunting to determine my truth and subsequently to determine my being.

Hauntings are very powerful and are created based on perceived negative events that take place in our life, and then how we decide to relate to those events. Once hauntings are set in, they become a powerful force and even a ruling force in your life. Hauntings are very real negative forces that can drive our decisions on a daily basis. They can become so powerful that they will build themselves in our bodies as strong emotions.

But these thoughts as hauntings are not who you are, but they are tied to you in such a way that determines your behavior. Let me give you another example of a haunting.

I have an aunt that is very eccentric, and she loves to try out of the way strange things. One day while visiting her in California when I was a little kid, she took my whole family out to dinner to a Parisian restaurant. Before then, I only ate basic traditional food: hamburgers, hot dogs, meatballs and spaghetti and the like. Once we reached home, the whole family was deathly sick. Everybody was throwing up. Needless to say, that was the last time we would allow our aunt to take us out to eat.

But since that time, whenever a new dish or an unrecognized dish was placed before me, I would reject it. Why? It was a haunting. Now again, the haunting within itself cannot be identified with who I am, but the resulting behavior pattern did determine who I was in the world. All this takes place in the Mind Field.

The Hauntings of the Mind Field

You are consistently bombarded by opportunities to increase and to move to higher levels, but when a haunting is your focus, you will miss pursuing your destiny by staying away from your most optimal roads. Also, when something great is placed in front of you, you will deny it due to hauntings.

Happy Haunting Home

Hauntings are structures within the Mind Field built by your own perceptions, and they come back as thoughts telling you or reminding you what can go wrong. Hauntings are literal places in the Mind Field that become a home to our consciousness and awareness. We literally live in the spaces of those places that exist in the Mind Field. To understand this further; you live in a house, but that house is not you. The haunting is a place and a thought pattern within the Mind Field in which you can live, but that place and space is not who you are.

Sometimes people can get so tied into their hauntings and their past troubles that they believe that that's the definition of who they are. The coolest thing about this is, because a haunting is a space within a place and is residential in nature, you can always move out at any time. In terms of improving your life, changing is not the order of the day, moving is. Many people try to change their lives, but all they need to do is move into a different space and place. Here's the structure:

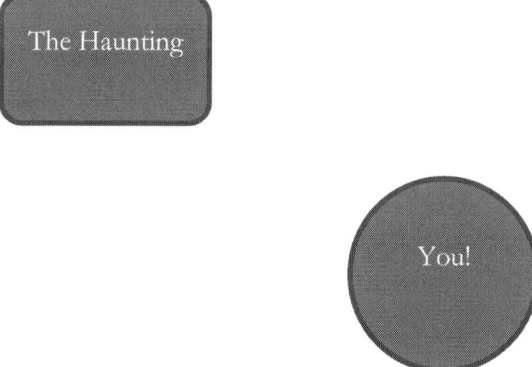

Notice here that the haunting is not in the same space and place that you are in. This is why I said, you are not your haunting, you are not what you experience, and you are not even the thoughts that are created. But you can be tied to them via the relationship that you have with that experience. The more conscious you are of a particular event, negative or positive; it determines your residence within the space of a place. It is the tying-in that I want to focus on here.

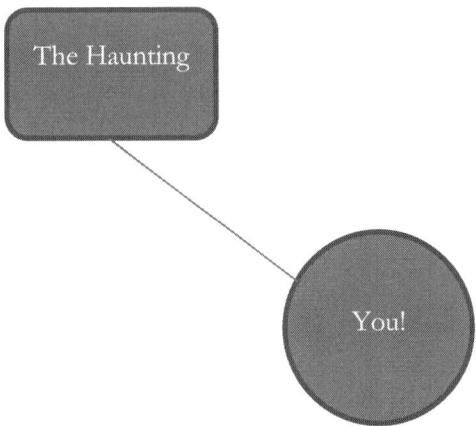

I want to call the line that ties you into your haunting a string, and this string can vibrate. As you focus or act based on a particular haunting, the string vibrates more and more. The more the string vibrates the more the haunting presents itself to you for consideration.

Now hauntings can come from many different circumstances and situations. The most prominent hauntings and likely hauntings come from childhood experiences. They can also come from a bad relationship or any bad experience. Hauntings can come from unfortunate events such as a car accident or a sickness. All of these are real events that present themselves as thoughts for consideration before you make your next move. Hauntings from the past can literally paralyze a person when it comes to decision-making.

Another major characteristic of a haunting is that it can be buried so deep, the haunting can seem to become part of who you are as a person. Every time you try to make a decision to move ahead, something seems to be stopping you. Most procrastination is blamed on laziness, but in fact, when somebody tries to move forward and make a decision

The Hauntings of the Mind Field

towards progression, a haunting or hauntings can show up in the decision, and then the movements and the decisions are now delayed or put off. What's haunting you?

In a lot of cases people just don't know. Hauntings are the secret negative thoughts and energy that can become such a normal part of a person's life, that addressing the reality of what haunts them at times is not found to be necessary. Then it can become a place of habitual comfort for them. People walk around every day with these monsters standing guard over their consciousness, and then the hauntings can manipulate the person's every move. This is one of the structures of the Mind Field. What's standing guard or ruling over your ability to move forward.

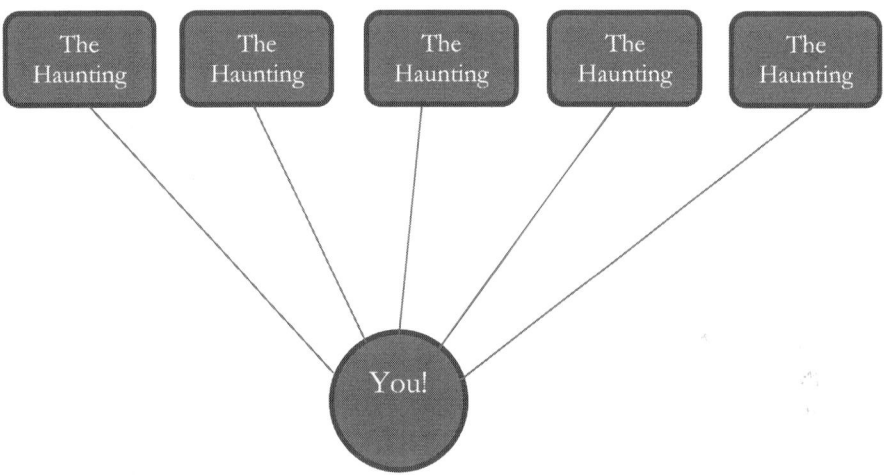

Here's an outline of the initial Mind Field, the hauntings, the strings, and you. There can be thousands upon thousands of hauntings that are created during a lifetime. Some of them you might be aware of, but most of them you are unaware of. Hauntings can be set by tragic events, such as a death of a loved one, a severe rejection, a highly disappointing moment in life, being raped or molested and the like. The hauntings can also be created by simple events that you might not even pay much attention to, such as, comments that might be made by someone that's negative, a small mishap, being fussed at by your boss, losing some money and the like. Many of these come back to play a major role in your decision-making and present themselves as hauntings.

Strings and Frequencies

There are always strings attached to every haunting, and you are in a relationship to every haunting forever because past events can never be erased. It is the attention that we might give a haunting, whether it be conscious or unconscious, that determines the rate of vibration of the string between you and that haunting. The strings like music play constantly in your life. Your choice is, is that you can choose the relationship to those strings, and then as they vibrate, it becomes the music of your life.

As I see people struggle with circumstances and situations in their life, generally I don't see the immediate event taking place, but I see the strings that are being played in their lives within that event, which is a representation of their past hauntings playing in their current circumstance. Most people try to deal with the event that's occurring in their life within that moment, but they never deal with the vibrating strings which leads them to experience that same event over and over again, because that is the song being played in their life stemming from the Mind Field.

Again, I feel it's more important to be attentive to the energy that takes place outside of oneself, even more so than what might be happening to them at the moment. Not only is it important to note the fact that the vibrations play a major part in our behavior patterns, but vibrations also present the fact that something lives on both ends of that vibration. This is a characteristic of vibrations. A vibration contains two active ends, and both ends are representative of you.

Vibrations are simply frequencies just like a television frequency, or a radio frequency. What exists on one end of a frequency also exist on the other end of the frequency, but in a different state. It's important to understand the difference between your state and your status. You never lose status, but your state changes as your energy changes. A television signal exists both at the TV station and on your TV at the other end simultaneously. A radio signal exists both at the radio station and your radio simultaneously at two different ends of the same frequency or vibration. A cell phone signal has your voice on the end where you are speaking, and then on the end where a person is listening simultaneously. You can be anywhere in the world, and this law will hold true. In much the same way, a haunting is not necessarily an event that happens on the two different ends, but it's you that exist on both ends of the frequency or vibration in two different states.

**You never lose status,
but your state changes as your energy changes.**

This is why I termed a haunting as a place, and you can choose to live in these places mentally, which gives rise to your experience in the same places physically.

Hauntings

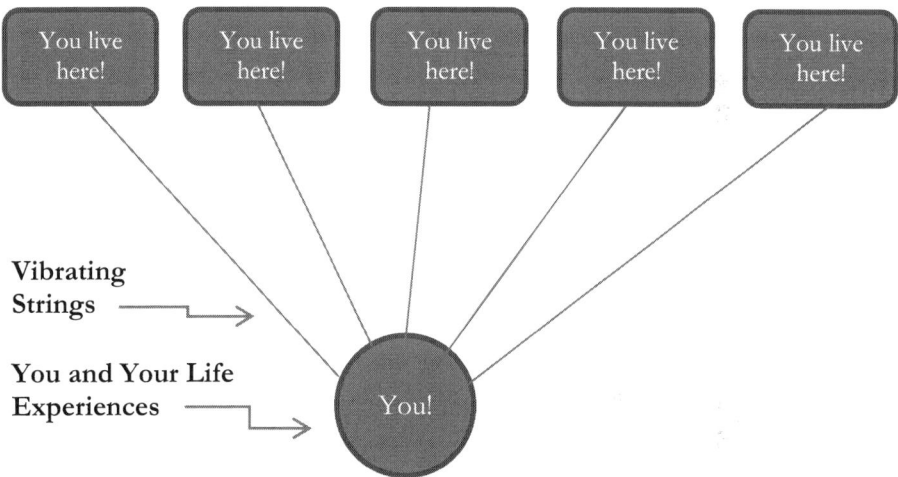

People have gone to church for many years trying to change their lives. People have paid thousands upon thousands of dollars to psychologist and psychiatrist trying to change their lives. People have gone to institutions of higher education trying to change their lives. People have abused substances for many years trying to change their lives. Change is just a religious concept when it comes to the Mind Field. It's not about changing; it's about moving to a different place in the Mind Field. This is paramount.

Hauntings are places in the Mind Field that stem from events that happen physically here on Earth. What else is there in the Mind Field where one can move on from a haunting space? Well there is another structure in the Mind Field called "The Callings". Let's take a look.

The Callings of the Mind Field

What I refer to as the "callings" are also places that exist within the Mind Field. The callings can be a little bit more difficult to understand, because our minds generally have been trained to deal with the negative. We must recognize the negative as a place in the Mind Field, and if there are places of negativity in the Mind Field that affect our lives, then there must also be places of positivity in the Mind Field that affect our lives. I define these places and spaces as "the callings". The callings shouldn't be harder to understand, they exist in the Mind Field just like the hauntings. They have vibratory strings in the Mind Field that are also tied to you. Callings are created just like the hauntings, but they come from a different place, a place of inspiration.

You can live in these places upon the awareness that these places exist. Now I'm not going to argue here the source of these callings. Most religions would say that it is God. A good number of other persuasions would simply refer to it as your higher self. Since both are one and the same, I don't think it makes a difference as to what it is termed, but I do want to prove that these places exist.

Everyone has had moments of inspiration, moments when they knew that they wanted to do something greater. Moments when life as it stands is no longer satisfactory and you want to live a better life. Moments when your job doesn't satisfy, and you are now thinking about moving up higher in the company, or you want to start your own business and make your own money. Moments when you begin to see more than what is seeable, and you feel it in your body.

Great inventors throughout history seem to pull amazing ideas from out of nowhere. They had the ingenuity to build great things where there has been no prior blueprint or model. Where does it all come from? What tells us to be who we are? Of course, it comes from "the callings". Now without further proof of this, I will map out for you the next part of the Mind Field. As you begin to see the structure more clearly, then the proof of the existence of the callings will become more apparent. These are places where you reside psychologically before things are manifested physically for your experience.

Callings

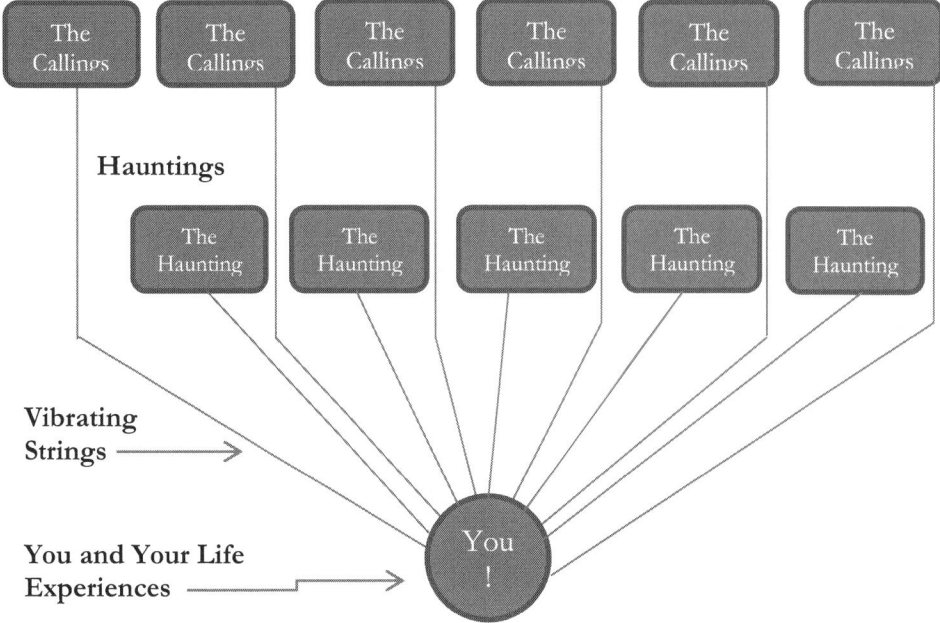

As you can see, the callings fall higher in the Mind Field than the hauntings. This does not denote that the callings in our lives are harder to achieve than the hauntings. Notice that there are strings that tie you to the callings as well as the hauntings. If you have any knowledge of how frequencies work, for the most part, distance is not a concern. As long as you are tied in, you have access. None of these strings can ever be broken. You can only determine which plays a greater role in your life – the hauntings or the callings.

For the most part, your involvement with the hauntings in your life will blind you towards the callings in your life. As the vibrations of the hauntings are heightened, the vibrations of your callings can be diminished. There is a calling and places that exist for every big idea, dream, and desire that you can muster up in your mind. The fact that they show up in your conscious mind proves that they exist. You don't need a preacher or a religious guru to help you to understand this simple fact. If a thought comes to your mind, it must exist. For every good thought that exist, there is a place and a space within the Mind Field that is the basis for that thought.

The Callings of the Mind Field

What you must understand as a fact is this; there are far more callings that are associated with your life than there are hauntings, but you must also understand that you can also live within the space of your callings. You do this by increasing the vibration of those strings that are attached to those particular callings.

Now what might puzzle people is this; why talk about vibrating strings that cannot be seen as if they are a real factor in life or a real factor in improving life? Let's take a closer look.

String Theories

Earlier we talked about two modes of tuning – Electronic Tuning and Musical Tuning. Tuning helps to align you with your hauntings and your callings. I will employ musical tuning to help you understand this point better. First, you must receive a quick music lesson and learn how strings are relevant in musical terms.

Note: Keep in mind at all times that strings are relevant to you and your hauntings and your callings'.

Because your hauntings and callings are places where you reside outside of yourself, I will refer to both from this point as House Chambers. Remember that "House Chamber" is a description of the places and spaces in the Mind Field, because these places and spaces become your mental homes. These homes are so real, that to understand them in any other way blinds you to the reality that the unseen is always responsible for what can be seen. Giving the places and spaces within the Mind Field the title "House Chambers", denotes the fact that the House Chambers are constructions, therefore completely within your ability to control.

Mind Field

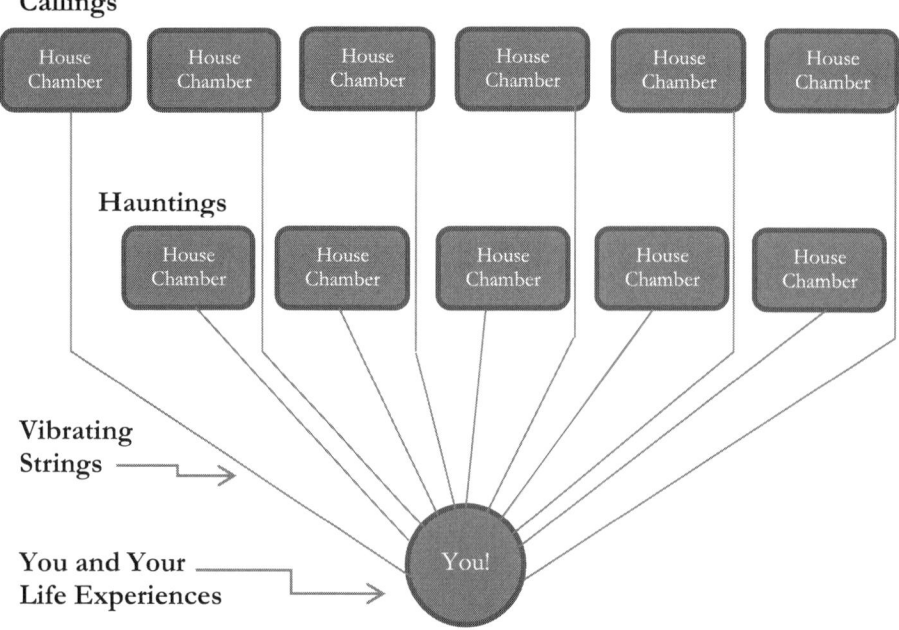

What exist between you and these house chambers are vibrating strings much like the strings on a musical instrument. A guitar has strings, a piano has strings, a violin has strings, and all these strings vibrate. When a note is played on these strings, it is the vibrations of a particular string that helps you to identify what note is being played by the sound you hear.

The Callings of the Mind Field

Modes of a Vibrating String

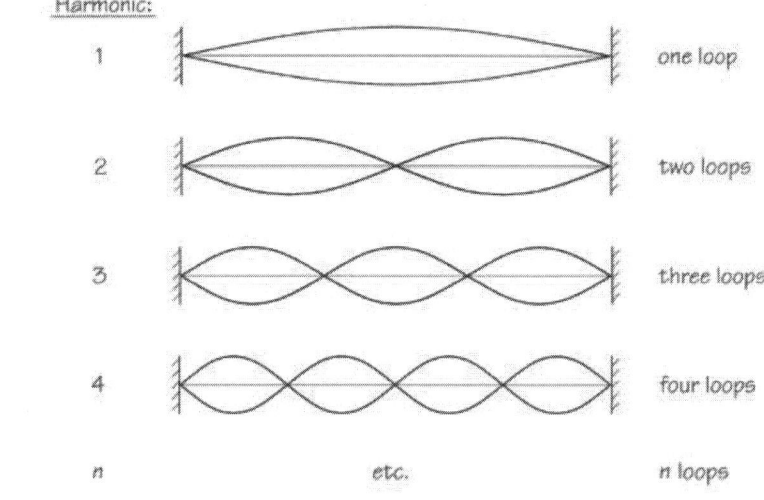

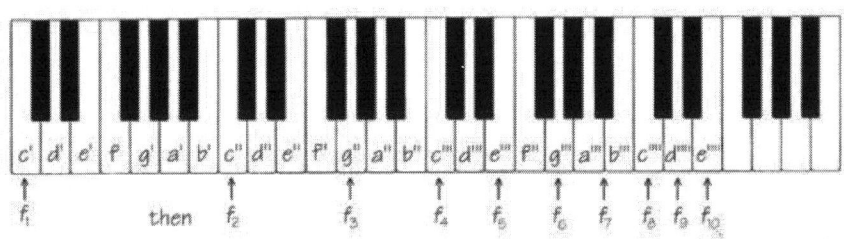

If the first harmonic of the string is tuned to middle C (c'), then the frequencies $f_2, f_3, \ldots, f_{10}$ correspond to the notes shown above.

Mind Field

To keep this simple:

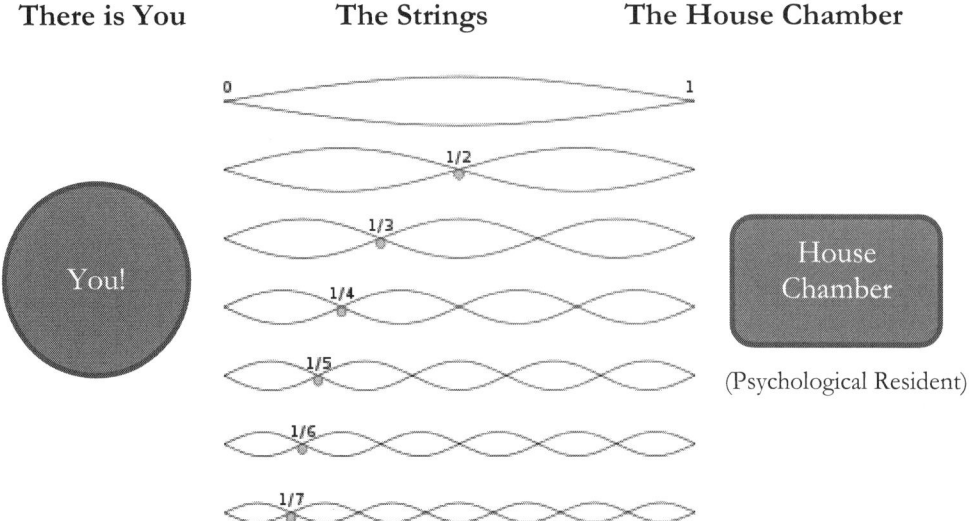

There is You   **The Strings**   **The House Chamber**

(Psychological Resident)

The strings vibrate between you and the house chambers. You must understand this as a fundamental part of the Mind Field and its structures. Between you and every thought that exist which belongs to you is a vibrating string. On both ends of the string the value of the "you" in the physical is drawn from the house you reside in. The house in which you reside is determined and can be identified by the rate of vibration of the string between you and the house you are mentally tied to. Just like when you hear a musical note, you can tell what that note is by its vibration; in life, your physicality is the vibration that is a witness to what's in your Mind Field. All creations are equal even though they differ in measure. One might create a successful business venture, the other might create a tragedy, but they are both creations equal in what it took to create them. Both are a witness to what was in the Mind Field.

Musical Tuning Strategies

Your first relation to the Mind Field is based on musical tuning, the adjustment of the strings between you and your house chamber. The

The Callings of the Mind Field

idea here is not to tune into your hauntings, but to tune into your callings. The greatest minds of all time were able to do this in order to manifest incredible lives and tune into things that literally changed human history. Some of the people that come to mind are Leonardo Di Vinci, Galileo, Joan of Arc, Pythagoras; and currently, Steve Jobs, Oprah Winfrey, Bill Gates, and Tyler Perry just to name a few. Most of these people had to draw great ideas in which they did not have a previous model to draw from. Where did it all come from? It all came from the Mind Field. They each answered their calling. They all lived their calling and made great contributions to mankind. How can this be you?

First, you must determine the sound or tone that comes from you. This is musical tuning. What was consistent about those I just mentioned, is that no matter what circumstances was presented to these people that could have easily become a haunting, they remained true to their calling. They kept doing what they were able to see within themselves, and then ultimately live and experience it outside of themselves.

Clear insight forces foresight.

Being clear about who they were gave them all the ability to see further than others around them. Having a great mind was not the source of their genius. Knowing who they were and what they wanted to do in life became the source of their genius.

Knowing who you are is the beginning of genius.

As they continued to behave every day based on their insight, their foresight became stronger and stronger. It was their behavior pattern that set the tone or the tune for what they wanted to accomplish. If there is something specific in life that you want to accomplish, you must tune your life to it by tuning your actions.

Here is what is special about this type of tuning. The more you become determined about what is sent out from you in terms of a consistent pattern, this pattern becomes your level of vibration. It then becomes easier at this point to recognize other callings, patterns, and vibrations that are consistent with your dreams. Then the hauntings that you might have been tied to becomes less of a focus and thusly diminished.

> **You don't have problems in life;
> you are only tuned into problems.**

This is the first benefit of musical tuning. The second benefit of musical tuning is that you are now able to identify those people that are in tune with your thinking. These people become your supporting cast or musically speaking, your fellow band members. It becomes hard to tune into the good things in life when you are surrounded by people who are out of tune. Here are the major strategies of musical tuning:

Strategies for Musical Tuning

1. Determine what you want in life and be clear about it.
   (Determine the note)

2. Act consistently towards your dream.
   (Stay in tune)

3. Build relationships that are consistent with your dreams.
   (Build a band)

4. Look past unhealthy patterns. Do not focus on the wrong.
   (Don't play the wrong notes)

5. Take measurement of what you do.
   (Be sure you are playing the right note)

Electronic Tuning Strategies

Now let's move over to electronic tuning. Electronic tuning works in a different way than musical tuning, but first, let's consider some types of electronics. You have cell phones, televisions, radios, and internet devices such as computers, and Apple Ipads. All of these electronic items work on the basis of frequency. Frequencies here are strings that work much in the same way as musical strings. All frequencies carry their own rate of vibration which in turn carries data from a source to a receiving device.

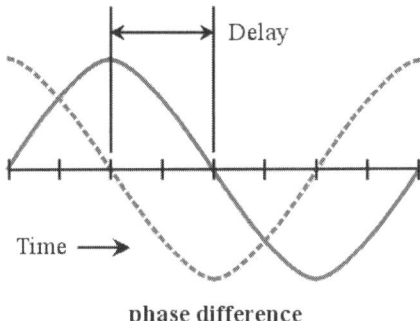

phase difference

Electronic frequencies are designed to carry specific data from one device to another. The key to receiving this data is your ability to tune into the frequency in which the data is being carried. Using television as an example, when you want to receive information from a specific television network, all you have to do is to tune into that channel by changing the channel from where you are currently to a new channel.

This sounds simple enough, doesn't it? Can you really change the channel from a haunting channel to a calling channel? Yes you can. Most people think of hauntings as a life standard. Many people consider the bad in life as a default, and the good in life as something to be achieved through hard work. This is far from the truth and people need to begin to understand life from a different perspective.

First of all, there is way more good that exist in the Universe than what we consider to be bad. There are more house chambers of callings than there are house chambers of hauntings. The issue here becomes a matter of what you're tuned into or the "channel" you are on. When you're tuned into the negative, it would appear that that's all there is on your psychological television. The programming in life seems to be limited to what can go wrong. This is because many people are unaware that the channels of callings our plenteous and are there to be selected.

Changing Channels

I am a little older. I lived in the time before cable television. When watching TV, we had three basic networks; ABC, NBC, CBS, and maybe even PBS, the public broadcasting network. That was it. What came on those channels is all you had to watch. In addition, at that time, the television networks went off at midnight. After a certain time, changing channels had no meaning. Then came cable and the cable networks. There's a cable network for almost anything you can think of. There is a network for food. There is a network for exercise. There is a network for science. There's a network for shopping. There is a do-it-yourself network. There is a home and garden network. There is a network for sports. There's a network for news. There's a network for adult entertainment. There's a network of shows just for children. Get the picture?

Sometimes we live as if there are no other options available in life. Consider what's available to you at the cable network, and then think in the same way for whatever you want in life; there's a station for that, there's a house chamber for that. You are not limited to the channels of what goes wrong in your life, but **you must become aware of all that exists in the energy network around you.** With this awareness you can choose to change channels, or move from an undesired house chamber (channel) to a house chamber (channel) that reflects a greater life.

House chambers that contain your callings are very accurate in delivering data. To understand this more, you have to understand the strings of frequency as it concerns electronic tuning. Electronic tuning is very accurate in its delivery of data. All frequencies or strings that carry data operate by strict laws and this is why scientists can rely on the technology of electronic frequencies without fail. Radio frequencies, television frequencies, Bluetooth frequencies, satellite frequencies, GPS frequencies are all severely accurate in delivering data. Airline pilots rely heavily on quite a few of these frequencies, and without them, a trip on an airplane can be very disastrous.

The Callings of the Mind Field

When you have a specific number on your cell phone, the frequencies that are aligned to get you to the cell phone in which you're calling is highly accurate. When you change channels on your TV for a desired station, you do not pick up other stations by accident. Whatever station you're tuned into, that's the data you will get. It works in much the same way when you want to tune into a house chamber that contains the information, data, or thoughts based on the great things and positive results you want in your life. You must change channels. You must dial the correct number. You must tune into what you want in life.

Interestingly enough, because we are dealing with electronic tuning, it denotes that the tuning has to be specific in order to receive the data that you want. You cannot tune into a haunting and a calling at the same time. Nor can you tune into a haunting and expect to receive data or thoughts from a calling. I used the terminology, "change the channel", but the terminology of "moving" is more accurate to use. You must move from one frequency to the other. Most people try to change the frequency in front of them or change the energy. To do this, you will wear yourself out, just move. Period! Move!

Get out of the pathway of bad frequencies! How do you know what and when frequencies are bad? If what is unfolding in front of you is not what you want, it's not the right frequency. Move!

One of the main characteristics of electronic tuning is not only are the tunings highly accurate, but they are extremely present. What do I mean by this? Your callings are not something that is developed; they exist in their entirety without you having to be concerned about making it what it needs it to be. Trying to develop a calling is like wanting to watch a certain type of movie and being worried about how to make the movie at the same time. When you know there's a great movie out there that you want to watch, you get a TV guide or pull up the channel guide that's provided by your cable company and you look for that movie. Once you find a particular movie that you desire, you "move" to the channel that carries the frequency that will deliver you that movie.

The movie is provided for you. Many people try to develop their dreams instead of moving to the channel in which their dreams exist. The problem lies in that many people do not have a personal TV guide developed that shows a life line-up of their desires. So, they watch whatever life channel that is presented to them.

Mind Field

If you never decide what you want, you'll never find what you want.

For every calling there is a frequency or a string that connects you to that calling. As I said, there are thousands upon thousands of hauntings that are created during a lifetime. But there are billions upon billions of callings that are available waiting for your selection. Hauntings will distract you from your callings if you're tuned into the hauntings. If what you want in life is not being delivered to you, you are simply on the wrong channel or tuned into the wrong frequency or string. You must bypass the hauntings and dial into your callings.

There are no losers in life, only choosers.

Strategies for Electronic Tuning

1. See more than what is seen, and then relate to the more and not the less.
2. Electronic tuning is not about changing, it's about moving.
3. Write out your personal TV Guide of life desires.
4. Callings are pre-developed for your enjoyment and exist in its entirety.
5. Accessing a calling is a choice. Select life experiences that match your programming.

Why We Tune

Humans are a special breed. Throughout the history of Earth's development, mankind ended up on top of the food chain. This makes us special. Behind everything that exists there is a thought that preceded that existence. For every plant, animal, mineral, and element, there is a thought behind it. As humans, we ended up at the far end of the chain of Earth's history. We ended up at the far end of the chain of creation. So behind who we are, there is a thought. What is this thought? How extensive is this thought behind you and I?

There is a special gene that is found in most mammals and humans. This gene is labeled as the FOXp2 gene. Only birds and humans contain a special mutation of this gene, which is called the language gene. So here alone, we can see that there were special considerations for human beings as concerning what thought is behind our existence. We were built with the special language gene that sets us apart from the rest of created existence. Let me tell you what I mean.

Language comes from adapted tones that are learned by hearing, internalizing, and then re-speaking. How this works in Finch songbirds, is that finches can hear specific tones and rearranges those tones into special melodies. But the finch has to receive those tones and internalize them before they can make a song. This is why birds have special melodies that they can sing so others can enjoy. What is unique here is that through the special mutation of the FOXp2 gene, finches are allowed to create something new at will. This makes songbirds a special creation.

Now in humans the FOXp2 gene plays a similar role. The FOXp2 gene gives humans the same power of arrangement. I have to tell you where and why this is important. You must note this fact and keep it in your mental vocabulary for future use. No other animal or any part of creation has the capability of arrangement. What does this mean? Every animal, insect, plant and mineral is responsive only to set pockets of commands extended to it by the environment. There is limited thought behind each of these forms of creation. Behind the "making" or reflecting of every human is unlimited thought, which makes you an unlimited being.

Let's look at this from a musical standpoint. When it comes to music, only birds and humans can take a series of notes and arrange them in the way that they want in order to make a melody. So their responsive system can take in information and then determine how that information is put back out. Other animals and species have a limited and a consistent responsive system to the environment, but humans are not tied to what happens in front of them as it concerns responsiveness. The environment doesn't necessarily have to dictate to us what we will be, but we can dictate to our environments as to what it will be. This is the power of arrangement. Just like birds can arrange a song, we have the power to arrange future life. The thought behind the human creation is that humans can continue to develop and arrange beyond their personal existence. This is the "You" that extends from "You".

This is the special gene that is given to us. Setting your environment is related to electronic tuning. You can move the channel of what you would like to receive. Musical tuning is more about determining what your life is going to be, so therefore you symbolically sing the tune of your desire by setting in order the life you want.

All animals and other species, being plant life or others, they eat what they eat, live where they live, produce what they produce, cycle in the time designed for them, and they have to be satisfied with that. Humans can look at what the environment is trying to dictate to them, and see beyond that something new and different, and then express it. This is vital. Don't miss this. In order for birds to create a song, they have to hear their notes to reproduce the notes into its own melody.

You and I, using the same gene mutation are enabled to see more than what is seen and create beyond what is seen. Most corporations consider this as innovation. The FOXp2 gene is built within us as a natural innovation tool. But where do you get the information for innovation? The notes have to exist in order for you to have something to arrange! In the same light, your callings have to exist in order for you to receive them via your frequency or string, and then you create based on your ability to innovate.

You don't see a spider that's called to build a web a certain way and then the spider decides to build a four-story web multiplex, complete with a shopping center for other spiders. You don't see ducks making fish sandwiches. You don't see cows making dinner plans. You don't see monkeys developing a business plan for a new Internet business. Get the point?

**See more than what is seen,
and then relate to the more and not to the less.**

The environment does not control humans. Humans carry this special gene to see what can't be seen and then produce it into the physical and create desired environments. The house chambers of your callings are there, but they must be tuned into. Nobody is ever poor in ideas when it comes to enhancing their lives. People are only poor in the choices that they make.

And so we tune. The construction material for our life melodies does not have to come from the events and circumstances that happen to us. We can pick up on entirely new material from the Mind Field. Then we can match up the evidence that we find in the physical that points to our mental creations. The supply for everything that you think is always there.

> **Nobody is ever poor in ideas
> when it comes to enhancing their lives.
> People are only poor in the choices that they make.**

The Gift of Looking Again

Here's the bottom line. We as humans are designed to look again. This is another gift provided by the FOXp2 gene. You have 12 notes on the piano, and every song that has ever been written came from these 12 notes. With these 12 notes, there are an infinite number of possibilities in music. 12 is the key to accessing infinite possibility.

You have the opportunity at times to repeat what's in front of you or to come up with new arrangements towards a greater existence. When you feel that you've reached a point where something "new" is not possible – look again. When you feel that you've reached a point where "better" is not possible – look again. When you feel that you've reached a point where the "greater" is not possible – look again.

The process of Imaging comes in handy at this point. Looking again starts with insight.

> **When people think of heaven, the tendency is to look up, but heaven is about looking in.**

Everything in the unseen is produced into the physical…and then the physical becomes the evidence of what can't be seen. This is what I can the Law of Evidence. Everything that is made is evident of the thoughts that existed before what was made became reality. For every thought, there is evidence of that thought. This is the law. All the current evidence of what exist now which can be seen proves this law. So for every thought that you have, you have to become proficient at recognizing the things that exist already that aligns itself with what you are thinking. Most people don't do this. They desire something, but then their immediate relationships that they create don't have anything to do with what they want. You have the sole responsibility to mirror what's outside of you with what exist inside you.

As I said earlier, insight forces foresight. People who focus long enough on what's inside them will have a better chance of finding the evidence outside themselves that correspond with what's in them. This is the process of Imaging. When things don't relate to your desires or they don't match your desires, look again. The evidence is there by law. It's never that it is not, but when you focus on something other than what's in you; it becomes entirely impossible to experience the evidence outside you. Look again. You always have the choice and the ability to choose your focus.

You also choose your relationships. It is the power of relationships that affect your foresight, so I outlined the 12 points of significance at the end of this book. You need these 12 points because they are much like the 12 notes on the piano. You need them for the melodies of your life and you need all 12 to reach a point of infinite possibility. Here they are:

To Be Viewed	**To Be Enriched**
To Be Comprehended	**To Be Advanced**
To Be Engaged	**To Be Rewarded**
To Be Praised	**To Be Exalted**
To Be Believed	**To Be Increased**
To Be Prioritized	**To Be Doubled**

These 12 points gives you the mental health that forces greater insight into all of life's possibilities. Without these 12 investments, it becomes difficult to tune into what's for you in life. The evidence for a great life is all around you, but you can't recognize these points of evidence when you are out of tune. The tune of the people around you becomes your song. Then your song or tune determines what you tune into outside of you. This is foresight. I also consider this to be one of the levels of authentication called Minor Authentication. Let's take a closer look at authentication.

The 4 Levels of Authentication

Authentication is the process of moving to the next level using the power of others who has your best interest at heart. It takes great relationships to do anything great, and it also takes others that have accomplished things before you to authenticate your direction.

1. **Minor Authentication**
2. **Major Authentication**
3. **Behavioral Authentication**
4. **Authentication by Accomplishment**

Minor Authentication is making sure that you establish the 12 points of significance around you, because these become the points of energy that supply your Mind Field with the balance needed to recognize other resources that are available to you that's needed for accomplishment.

Major Authentication is provided when you relate to a person or persons that have accomplished what you are looking to accomplish. This can be in the form of a mentorship, or studying materials that are related to your goals. This saves you time and helps you to "Push Time" by soliciting the energy of those who have experienced completion in your area of interest.

Behavioral Authentication is setting a daily regimen that is consistent to your vision.

Then you are authenticated by your own accomplishments. Nothing else authenticates you more than when you get results. You have to gather your past results and put them in front of you. You can

Mind Field

also do this by creating lists of gratitude. Be thankful for the things you have done and accomplished in the past. This adds tremendous value.

You can use the first three levels of authentication to get results, as this will help you to push time. Time is your friend, and you want to use time as an ally to accomplish your goals. In reality, instead of accomplishing things in time, you want to have time to deliver your results for you.

Keys to Pushing Time

This is the concept of taking your dreams, your goals, and your destiny and tying it into the seasons and cycles that is initiated by the relationships that you build using the process of authentication which powers you towards accomplishment at greater speeds.

1. **Determine your destiny or goal.**

2. Under each house chamber you have to set the energy for production.

3. **Use the 12 points of significance, but relate these to your specific project or goal.**

4. Use the first three levels of authentication.

5. **Push Time using Major Authentication**

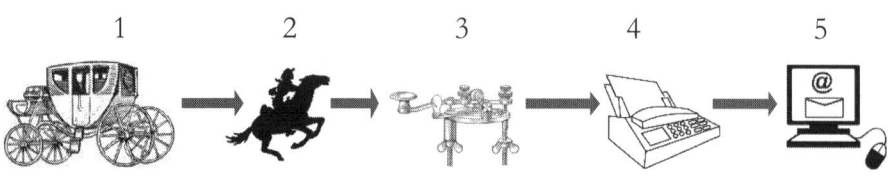

Horse & Carriage   Pony Express   Telegraph   Phone & Fax   Email

The Callings of the Mind Field

What you have here are different modes of accomplishing the same goal, and that's the goal of delivering a message. Consider what you are trying to accomplish, and your ability to accomplish your goal is at a level 1 or 2. 1 takes several days and 2 takes about a day. 3 takes a whole afternoon. 4 and 5 are instantaneous. If you can find someone that has accomplished what you want to accomplish, they are a 5 to you. Having a person who can authenticate you that is a higher skill level will shorten your time frame of effort. It's like pushing your efforts through his or her knowledge, and then your 1 or 2 becomes a 5 as it concerns time.

Your 1   Processed through the experience of others   Becomes a 5

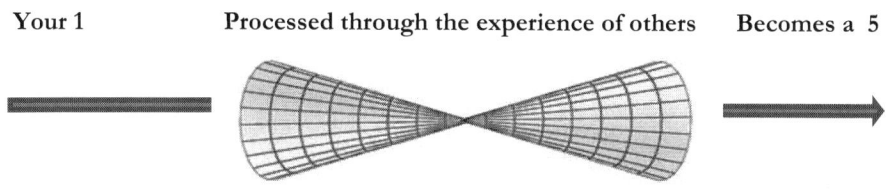

The energy of the work that has been done before you by someone else is an actual existence. This is usable energy. You absorb the energy of what has been accomplished before and not repeat unnecessary processes. Again, you do this through mentors, books, videos etc. By having a person who has accomplished what you want to do to authenticate you, helps you to push time as you travel through their previous experience. As you travel through their experience, you pick up on their completions and move through their spaces and places in the Mind Field. You essentially push time using someone else's success. This is tuning into success

Once your house is built, the energy is set, and your levels of authentication are created, you automatically enter into a cycle or season. When the cycles and seasons are set, they behave in much the same way as all other cycles and seasons that you might be familiar with that existed from the beginning of time.

The more you repeat this process, you begin to learn how to shorten the cycles and seasons as you build better relationships and teams for success.

This is a system of how things work in time work anyway. Notice how things in nature and things within the universe unfold. It uses the same system of creating relationships and setting its energy in order to unfold into the next stage, the next level, or into something new. Why does it work? It is congruent with many other systems of relationships and timing, such as the conception of a baby, which is a result of a relationship, then the birth, which is then timed out into a 9 month cycle.

All relationships spawn cycles. This is the key. This is the secret. So, when you are building or setting your first house chamber, make this your motto:

There is only ONE thing I'm doing.

This becomes paramount to your ability to grow exponentially as your patterns unfold!

You need the first in order to birth the second!

Tune into your callings...!

The Four Components of the Mind Field

The four components of the Mind Field are as follows:

1. **Relationship**
2. **Rationale**
3. **Regimen**
4. **Results**

Each of these four components are highly reflective of one another. The bottom line here is to get to the results.

Results are reflective of your regimen.

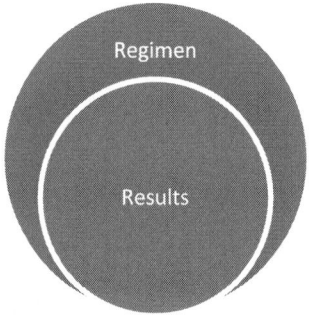

Your regimen is reflective of your rationale.

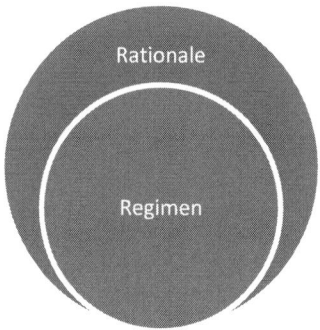

Your rationale is reflective of your relationships.

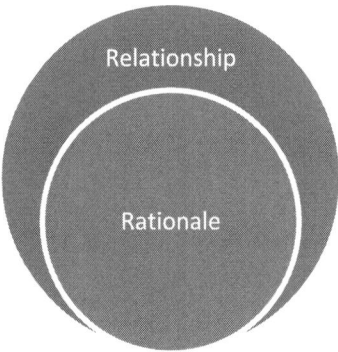

So all are closely related and highly reflective of one another and work together as a unit.

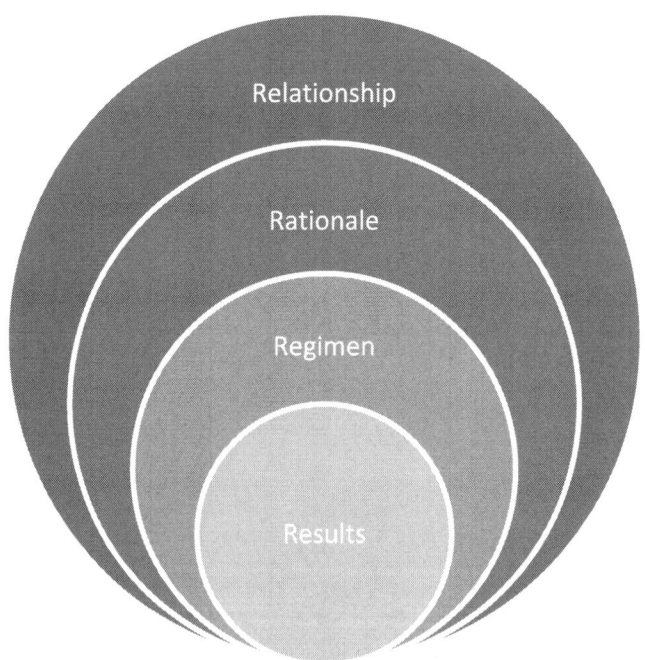

The Four Components of the Mind Field

Let's look at definitions and the association of each component.

Relationship

Relationship is the foundation in which the Mind Field is built upon. Without building the proper relationships around you, it becomes hard to maintain a decent mindset to navigate the Mind Field. Relationship leads to rationale and mental health.

Rationale

Rationale is how you think. Rationale is the mind processes used to navigate the Mind Field. It is also the quality of your thinking. Rationale in turn determines your behavior pattern.

Regimen

Regimen is your behavior pattern. It stems from your rationale or your mode of thinking. The quality of your thinking determines the quality of your regimen. A solid regimen according to the Mind Field produces good results. Regimen is simply your daily actions.

Results

Results are the completion of your desires. Results stems from a good regimen that is practiced every day. Results then become the institution or the monuments in which you can form even greater relationships to begin the process over again.

So as you see, these four are highly reflective of one another and deeply intertwined with one another. You cannot have a good mind without the relationships that make the mind good. People say all the time, that this person or that person or persons drove me crazy or made me sick. This is a very true statement. A stable mind comes from stable relationships. So relationships are paramount to anybody's success. So let's take a look at the first component of the Mind Field, relationship.

Relationships

How people treat you and act towards you has more of an impact on your haunting and callings than anything else. What you think plus your relationship equals your energy. The key to any good relationship is agreement, and one of the most important factors of your relationship is the ability of the people that are around you to see who you are. People must see and understand who you are in order to agree with your destination. You cannot surround yourself with persons who lack understanding, first in general, and most importantly who lack understanding as to who you are and what you want in life. When you surround yourself with these kind of people, they represent your fear and not your focus.

People who choose to have sorry people around them are generally afraid of their own destiny.

Personal Statement to Others: The moment you see me or come into my personal space, plan to make that moment successful for me, because I will be sure to be conscious of doing the same for you.

Whatever you think doesn't come alive until you build *working* relationships around it.

You have to be concerned about the energy you build around you, and the greatest energy created around you is created through the relationships you build. The quickest way to bad results is forming bad relationships. It works the same when it comes to business; the quickest way to bad results is to form bad teams.

The Four Components of the Mind Field

Again, some relationships are representations of your fear, some habits are representations of your fear, and all unfortunate circumstances are molded and modeled presentations of your fear. So people and your relationships should be your first priority and level of management.

The word fear and the word shame are primarily the same word and sometimes shame becomes the basis of how you build your relationships. So let me tell you what shame is. Shame is when you don't recognize who you are. It's when you don't give yourself proper value. It's when you reduce yourself in your own thinking so then you begin to base decisions off of this low evaluation of yourself. Subsequently, based on this type of evaluation, more relationships are built. What we don't recognize, because of the accuracy of the Mind Field, when relationships are built on shame, it will always produce shameful results.

So first, you must construct a design based on your desire. Next, the people around you have to match your design based on your desire, which then becomes your destiny. When you choose people based on shame, you birth more disappointments rather than building and creating more good results.

Relationships also reflect your perception. What you want to do is to have like-minded people around you. It becomes very hard to reach your destiny when everyone around you is not on the same page. Another way to put it in terms of electronic tuning, you must have people watching the same channel you are watching. There's nothing like a good fight over life's remote control. You must take in consideration that you want relationships that are going to take you somewhere and take you where you want to go.

This might seem a little selfish at first, but you must realize that the four components of the Mind Field -relationships, rationale, regimen, and results, are very scientific and energy accurate, and if the people you invite around you are not destiny oriented, you will lose in the end, and this is guaranteed. Your relationships reflect into your mindset. This is also a science and a law. Let me explain.

There is no mind without relationship. To explain this, I want to give you the four components of relationships, in which I call "Action Exchanges". They are as follows:

1. Investment
2. Integrity
3. Intimacy
4. Increase

4 Action Exchanges

Without these four components you don't have a relationship. I gave you 12 earlier, but these four are more action oriented, and is also the basis for creating real and usable energy for positive development. Again relationships are crucial, and the results of relationships should be measured at all times. When you find yourself not going anywhere, I can guarantee you that it has everything to do with the people you associate with and are closely tied to.

Significance

To have people interested in you is very important. To have attention, touch, and somebody who is hands-on is vital to your personal energy dynamics. It is also important to have relationships with this type of focus when it comes to accomplishment.

When you accept diminished behavior towards you, you are practicing poverty.

The Four Components of the Mind Field

You can only push time based on the number of people that are interested in you, interested in what you are doing, and also interested in what you have to offer. When you have the proper people around you, you have the basis and the ability for proper exchanges. These proper exchanges will form the basis of your initial economy, which will then incite incremental and exponential growth. When you accept improper or diminished actions towards you, you are also practicing the denial of the fact that there are people out there that will treat you right. The words money and mind have the same history, so it becomes impossible to live a great life without a solid mental economy. True economics starts with who's around you.

1. Investment

Everything in life exchanges in order to live. There is no life without exchange. It takes quality exchanges for things to grow. So the first part of relationship is about the investments we make into one another.

The people around you must invest into you.

I always say that there is no such thing as self-esteem. Which is true. All of our esteem comes from others. Everyone, no matter how much of an opinion that they might have about themselves, that opinion is not validated until somebody agrees with you. I call this the process of authentication. Everyone needs to be authenticated in life, and when you surround yourself with people that don't authenticate you, you lose value just as a stock on the US stock exchange loses value when it is not authenticated by an actual value.

Doctors don't become doctors until they are authenticated by somebody who became a doctor before them. Lawyers will not become lawyers until they are authenticated by a lawyer who became a lawyer before them. It is hard for a male child to become authenticated without a father investing into that child's manhood. It is hard for a little girl to become a woman without a mother seeing the womanhood in the girl and telling her that she is a wonderful woman. These are all investments. You must have people investing into your direction in order to authenticate your direction.

You might have in mind that you're definitely going to accomplish a specific goal, but if you surround yourself with people that are ignorant of your passion, you will find yourself never reaching that goal because it's hard to build a mind towards what you desire when you have people around you that are mindless towards who you are.

2. Integrity

Completion is always the order of the day. Life is about completion. Life is about results. Without results there is no measurement or foundation to move on to what's next. Here integrity is vital. What is completed in your life? When a person makes a commitment to you, that commitment registers in your mind as a completed item. That's just how the mind works. What happens when people don't follow through on their commitment? Your mind registers a great disappointment. A disappointment in the Mind Field is very unhealthy. As matter of fact, it is quite dangerous.

Remember how I stated earlier how we as humans can draw from the Mind Field to create wonderful lives and that we a have a specific gene, the FOXp2 gene to do this? What happens to the Mind Field when it is filled with disappointments? These disappointments become hauntings, and the more you surround yourself with these types of disappointments, you will only be left with hauntings to build the songs of your life. How horrible!

The reason why integrity is so important is, you need to get used to hearing things being said, and then seeing those same things being done. This creates a pattern, and a pattern creates a frequency or string. Yes. People's commitments to you become house chambers and strings in the Mind Field, and unfulfilled house chambers become hauntings that become resulting patterns in your life.

Never get used to people telling you one thing and then doing another thing. This is the most horrible form of relationship that you can allow around you. Like I said, it becomes very dangerous. You might be sitting and wondering, I've done all I can to make things work in my life, but I cannot seem to reach my goals. I can almost guarantee you, it is not anything that you're doing, it's the people that you associate with. As cold as it might sound, you need a system of requirements for the people who want to be your friend, associate with you, or work with you.

3. Intimacy

When I think of intimacy, I'm not necessarily talking about sexual intimacy. Here, I am talking about the power of engagement and the power of attention. This is the power of being involved and the power of knowing that somebody cares about what you want. This is the basis of true intimacy. Deep involvement. Nothing happens without agreement, but in addition to that, there are no results without action towards these agreements. That's why integrity is important, and intimacy should run close behind commitment.

First of all, attention is vital. You cannot have people in your life that can't invest the proper level of attention needed for authentication. There are people that have a systemic existence of friends around them that are shallow and couldn't make a decision towards what you want to do, even if you paid them. These type of people need to be eliminated from your life. Intimacy is not only about the attention received, but the resulting actions based on that attention.

This happens to women a lot. Men can give the highest attention with verbal acclamations and proclamations. For some women, this becomes enough; he said it, and I feel good about it. So then their personal value is based off of words and not action. Intimacy is about words and actions.

I have broken down intimacy further into four components. They are as follows:

1. **Consciousness**
2. **Communication**
3. **Connection**
4. **Commitment**

Consciousness is about attention. You cannot have unconscious people around you. Even a conversation with that type of person will be bad. These people will always be asking,

"What are you talking about?",

"What did you just say? I don't understand that."

"What did you just do? I don't get you."

So on and so on…

Conversations with these people become very difficult because they are unconscious of your drive towards your destiny. You can say let's go in one direction, they will say, no let us go in this direction. Not only will your conversation be strained, but all of your movements will be strained also.

You need people that pay attention. You need people that offer good communication and understanding. You need people who know how to connect. You need people around you that know how to stay committed to optimal direction.

You cannot have persons around you that are psychologically distant from you.

Lacking any of these things will eventually show up in your rationale or your mind. People will ask you, what is wrong with you? You might not even know. But I can tell you, it's the relationships that you build.

4. Increase

Let's go back again to the FOXp2 gene. Why do we have this gene? Increase. Life for mankind is not about survival like other animal kingdoms, but life for mankind is about increase. The purpose of having a mind or a gene to be able to see more is simply to have more. None of what you see around you that is man-made, did not pop into existence without somebody being able to think of it first. Where did that thought come from? Think of every invention that you can imagine. You can think of these inventions after-the-fact of their creation. The imagination of the inventor came before-the-fact of the creation.

So evidently this gene allows us to see "more", and then it allows us to arrange. Without this gene we would not be human. So without the callings in the Mind Field, we would not be human. Monkeys don't have the privilege of deciding to be able to fly. But a man can look into the sky and say, I would like to fly one day. The Mind Field doesn't stop there. Man at this point can now begin to picture what it might take for him to learn to fly, and then he can take action based on his perception. Where does all of this come from? The Mind Field. Answering your callings is about increase. Not only for yourself, but for others who get to benefit from your insight.

Answering who you are is about increase.

You are designed to increase. You are designed to grow. But it all starts with a thought. Every thought has a house chamber, and every house chamber has a frequency or a string tied to you. So again, agreement is paramount. All of your relationships should lead to some type of increase, whether it is a personal relationship or a business relationship.

Rationale

Trust me. Your relationships flow right into your rationale. Your relationships are the construction materials for your mind. Without the right relationships, your rationale can become very thin. Have you ever been at the point where you said to yourself, I can't think? This is because of the energy that is set around you has become a bad environment for thinking.

Perception is the highest gift given to humankind. It allows anyone who is facing a situation or a circumstance that they don't like, to revamp it using their perception. This goes back to the concept of innovation. Innovation is the ability not only to assess what's wrong before you, but also to look at what's new that exists beyond what's in front of you. It takes a powerful mind to do this. It takes optimum rationale to do this.

Innovation, powered by the FOXp2 gene is a gift given to anyone who's facing what may seem to be a tragedy, downfall, or a disappointment. What's really being faced is an opportunity for the mind to do its thing. Because of the mind, there is no such thing as dead ends. There is always something "more". There is always something new. This is where you can change your expectations and not have your expectations to suffer at the point of shame and fear. Let me tell you something about the mind that you might not know.

The mind needs results to know that it exists. Hence, the need for substance. You need to have results and accomplishments in order to know that you exist. Results are the ultimate form of authentication. That's why I said earlier, that completion is important. The word mind, the word think, the word mint, and the word money all come from the same root word, which is –mon. So, to think is to create or mint something into existence. This is why results become vital to the mind. The mind becomes crazy and unstable without accomplishment.

Having good rationale is about proving the mind by creating what is thought of. When a man sees a beautiful woman, he begins to dream and desire all the possibilities of what can be. He imagines it and he can even feel it within his body what the results would feel like. Now, what is within his mind has to be authenticated. But if the woman doesn't give him any attention, and without that attention the mind cannot reach completion. In order for authentication to take place, an agreement must be reached, and it is within that agreement plus corresponding action that things are completed. That's why I said, it is rough going when you have people around you that cannot consistently agree with you or be attentive towards you. Things don't get done.

The mind needs completion to know that it is alive. A properly constructed mind based on great relationships, turn out good actions that lead to great results. So again, as these four are highly reflective of each other: relationship, rationale, regimen, and results, you need to make sure that you have solid rationale to build a consistent regimen.

What you think or what comes to your mind (money) is valuable. I tell people all the time, never disregard what comes to your mind. Sometimes it's better to disregard the people around you who think differently from you than to disregard what comes to your mind.

Deleting Fear

Shame is the enemy of the mind. So how do you get rid of shame and then the resulting fear, which clearly blocks the mind and leads to unhealthy relationships? First, you do not need to overcome fear, because fear only stems from shame, which is a low evaluation of yourself and your abilities. Shame is simply a haunting of misinformation about yourself. This misinformation stems from a connection that's informing you as to who you are. This information is just that, a line of information, but not facts. It only becomes a fact when you act on it.

Notice, you act on it. Truth is about what is acted on. So here, you change your truth by determining what you respond to. You are smart enough to know, even if you are telling yourself, when information that you receive is not optimal. When it is not, you must keep an ear out for the correct information. Choosing correct information about yourself should come from inspiration. Fear is only a monitor. If fear exist, it simply means you are hearing wrong and seeing wrong. Stop. Listen, and look again for the right information. When it is right, the fear will dissipate. Only then should you act.

Let me back you into a corner. There is always a price to pay for shame. With shame, any and everything returned to you will come up short, screwed up, unbalanced, unfair, unfortunate, uncomfortable, and the like. Misinformation as to who you are keeps you in the wind. Not acting on "the best You", keeps you in the wind. Things slip through your fingers, you run out of resources when you need them most, and you continuously miss out on the opportunities to advance.

Shame secretly points out what you don't deserve, so when better opportunities are presented, you can't even recognize it. You don't move when the time is right, and when you are faced with a challenge, all that registers in your body is fear. You also give yourself away and call it helping people, but in the end you are drained. This is the price of shame!

This is never who you actually are, it's only what you choose to see. Look again if needed until you get it right. Get in the habit of seeing your true self correctly. The better, stronger, smarter, wiser, and greater you is always present.

1. Choose to only hear correct information about yourself, especially when it comes from you.
2. If it's not right – look again. There's always something "more" beyond any current presentation.
3. Act only when it's right.
4. Die to what's old and what's not working. Let it go.

Regimen

Regimen is simply the actions that you take daily that are based on your rationale. Again, without good rationale you cannot form a good regimen. Have you ever wondered why people procrastinate? Simply, they don't have the energy around them to move forward. Remember how I said that your thoughts plus relationships equals your energy. Procrastination is never about what you want to do, it's always about the energy that you have to do what you want to do. You cannot link your thoughts with someone with a lack of investments and integrity towards you and expect to get rolling in life. It will never happen, because the energy is simply not there to motivate you to act consistently towards your destiny.

Again, regimen is about actions. It is what you do daily, and what you do daily determines your results. All of this stems from the mind, and the energy created. Like I said, each of these four components is highly reflective of the other. When you find yourself unable to complete the right actions, it is simply because you don't have the mind to do it. Which by the way, having the wrong mind repeats into never having the right money to get things done. For the most part, when you don't have the mind to do something, it is because of the relationships that draw on you in a negative way and pulls at your mental energy.

If you want to complete an exercise program, stay around some people who exercise every day and I guarantee after a while you will begin to soak in the energy of exercise. This is a science and not a philosophy. This is something that you can take lightly and then expect to do the things in life necessary to be successful.

Results

Results are important. As I said earlier, without results, it becomes impossible to know your own existence. Results are paramount. Everybody wants results. Everybody wants good results. Good results are possible and can be attained more consistently when you use the Mind Field.

There are two types of results: results that come from your thinking, and then the results that happen to you at random when you don't think. Remember, thinking and money comes from the same root word, so how you think is your first crack at financial opportunity. Thinking is paramount to your success. A closer look allows you to know that in reality, thinking and results are one and the same thing. Results become important because it is results that become the monuments in which you and others can glean new goals, desires, and ideas.

How you think is your first financial opportunity.

Results are evident of your thinking and without evidence of your thinking; it becomes hard to get a sense of validation or authentication. I can give you an outline of how to get results, but results become automatic when you follow the first three components of the Mind Field. If results are reflective of your regimen, and your regimen is reflective of your rationale, and your rationale is reflective of your relationships, then creating the right relationships, thinking with the right rationale, and then having a consistent regimen will give you guaranteed results. All four components are one and the same thing. So let's map it out one more time.

1. Determine what your dreams and destinies are to be, and then build your relationships accordingly.

2. Secondly, be sure to maintain a clear rationale, which will help you to identify your callings and diminish your hauntings. Good relations are the foundation for a good mind. Get rid of shame, reevaluate yourself as needed.

3. Third, make sure that your actions are consistent with what's on your mind. If your actions are not consistent with what's on your mind, then they are consistent with what's on the mind of others.

4. Forth, make sure that your results line up with your dreams and destinies. If not, begin a relationship check, a rationale check, and a regimen check. Fix these, and you can fix your results.

Relationship → Rationale → Regimen → RESULTS

The Time and Timing of the Mind Field

The Mind Field is about mastering accomplishment. What you want to do here is to take the structures of the Mind Field and the components of the Mind Field and then outline them in a way that you can use the Mind Field system to accomplish what you want in life. For the most part, knowing what you want to accomplish is not an issue, but the "knowing" exist in the Mind Field and you must become proficient at moving what you know to what is produced outside of the Mind Field.

We will deploy one of the greatest Mind Field tools that guarantees production of your dreams and the reaching of your life's destiny – Time.

Everyone on earth is equally rich, but not everyone accesses his or her riches equally. There is never an economic difference between persons, there is only a mind difference which is then reflected economically. Now to help you discover the value of time as it concerns accomplishment, let's remind ourselves of the structures and components of the Mind Field, and then add in the element of time.

> **Everyone on earth is equally rich on earth,
> but not everyone accesses his or her riches equally.**

The Structures of the Mind Field

1. The Mind Field always starts with **You**.
2. Extended from you are **Strings** or **Frequencies** tying you to **House Chambers** within the Mind Field.
3. You control the strings via two types of tuning - **Electronic Tuning** and **Musical Tuning**
4. You have House Chambers attached to the far end of each string - **The Hauntings** and **The Callings**.
5. You have the **Components** – **Relationship, Rational, Regimen,** and **Results**

6. You have the **Authentications – Minor, Major, Behavioral, Accomplishment**
7. You set the **Energy** of the **Strings** or **Frequencies** by fostering the needed **Relationships** and **Authentications**.
8. **Consistent Actions**
9. **Cycles** and **Seasons** are created and set for your desires and destiny.
10. What is heightened in the Mind Field is then produced in the physical.

Now to get to accomplishment and the results, we must add into the mix the element of time. Everything in life works according to cycles and seasons. The basic cycles and seasons bring certain results and have done so for billions of years. We can witness these results as they are guaranteed based on the timing of these results. Another thing that is guaranteed is time itself. Time comes and goes whether you like it or not.

When I mentioned the fact that everyone on earth is equally wealthy, time is one of the items of wealth that is taken into consideration. Everyone on earth shares the same amount of time every day. The sun rises and sets daily the same for everyone. So we all share the wealth of time, which is guaranteed for everybody. Along with this guarantee of time, we all see that the cycles and seasons bring guaranteed results, and we can set our expectation of those results with a very reasonable sense of confidence. What we want to do here is guarantee your results in much the same way by using cycles and seasons.

The Perks of Time

Let's start with some basics. The sun circles the earth every 24 hours as the earth rotates on its axis. The earth rotates around the sun once a year. The moon has its monthly cycles. The star space of the zodiac system has 12 placements in the sky every 365 days. These are the basics that deal with the sun, the moon, and stars. As time passes, these celestial existences repeat themselves within cycles and consistently supply the same results.

There are other cycles and seasons that are easily recognized which embed themselves within nature, biology, and science. You have the four seasons: summer, fall, winter and spring. Then you have animals and humans that live within patterns of existence based on a combination of celestial cycles and cycles within nature. Some birds fly north and south at specific times of the year. Women have their monthly cycles based on the moon cycle. There are cycles within science, such as electrons spinning around the nucleus of an atom and frequency cycles within the light spectrum. These are some basic cycles that we all know and understand that operate based on time, and as time cycles around you see the results within these cycles.

One thing that is guaranteed, is that time does not stop for anyone. So time within itself is a guarantee. What you want to do here is to make time your ally so it can bring you results just as it does every day in so many other different levels. You have to make time your friend, because time will always be the key to accomplishment and achieving any results. Another important cycle to note here is the conception and birth of a child. Generally, after a child is conceived, in 9 months you will see the result of the conception within the general cycle that has existed for hundreds of thousands of years. Here again, time plays a vital role in the delivery of results. Right relationship with time brings results.

Results and Time

All results based on your desires and planned destinies must be set in time. Here, I'm not talking about building a plan of action, but allow me to introduce you to a way of associating what you want to accomplish and the results you want to achieve that might be a little bit outside of the box, but yet it pulls on a little bit of science. This system is easy to comprehend, and you should be able to find your way to accomplishment and reaching your goals more consistently.

First, we must start with this fact: you cannot plan to be successful; you can only build memories within your body of being successful, which in turn will produce the success you are looking for. So what you are doing differently here is you are not setting a bunch of dates and deadlines, nor will you be creating a plan of action. You start by building houses or better stated, building house chambers. House chambers become memory that stores in your body. Once the house chambers are in place, you can set each chamber in time to produce the physical results, and then time becomes responsible for delivering the results, just like time delivers so many results that are currently based on more recognized cycles and seasons. I call this – pushing time.

What is the secret of time doing the work? Notice I did not say, "Doing the work in time", but have time do the work for you! Time is designed to do the work, not you. Here, I don't want you to think of time in terms of dates and deadlines or what you judge and determine by your watch, but think of time in terms of cycles and seasons. When you create the memory in your body, time will then replay what's created in you.

The energy you create will shorten time.

What you want to do here is take your efforts, your projects, your goals, your desires, your business, or your destiny and define its cycles and seasons. Then use the power of the energy you create to shorten the cycles and seasons. This is a process that has consistently happened in history many times over.

First you must become great in your first space or house chamber that exists within your overall goal. Take full responsibility for taking what you have at your disposal, no matter how small, and doing it well. Things naturally grow off of success. After success, time will always have the next thing waiting for you.

Time is designed to do the work of delivery of results, not you.

Here are the Basics

1. Do not create a plan of action. Build a house, a House of Accomplishment.

2. Identify what you would like to accomplish and break it down into 4, 8 or 12 part units. Each one of these units will represent a house chamber.

3. You must energize each one of these units or house chambers by executing profitable relationships by the process of authentication. This will help with setting your frequency or string tie-in to these house chambers.

4. Now you can set each house chamber in time to achieve your results. To do this, you must push time in front of a natural cycle or season. It's just like planting a seed; you have to plant it within the right cycle. The same works when a child is conceived, you see the results brought about by time.

As you can figure, if you're setting desires, you're not going to plan to build a house that's a haunting or a haunted house. You want to build a house based on your calling. Now what else is indicative of time is that things can remain the same over time or grow exponentially over time. So what you want to focus on here is the growth that can take place over a period of time in your Mind Field. So focus on your calling.

You must focus on the rate of vibration of each string. You control the vibration of the strings to your respective house chambers by the relationships you build, the rationale you use, and the regimen you practice. Everything must be consistent to the house chamber you set. If you want to see the results from a particular chamber, make sure that the components of the Mind Field are consistent, and that they properly reflect one another.

To set time you must push each house chamber in front of a cycle or a season or through somebody else's cycle or season. It is at this point that time takes over the production of your results and delivers accomplishment. Pushing house chambers in front of time has to do with the relationships you build with potential mentors or people who can authenticate you. Here you have to form a relationship with someone who has accomplished what you're looking to do. This is simply a type of mentoring process and the process of authentication.

The Nuts and Bolts of the Mind Field and Accomplishment

Here are the four practices you would need to focus on:

Building the House

Energizing the House

Authenticating the House

Achieving Accomplishment

These four practices must be done for each house chamber that you build within the House of Accomplishment. Remember, you set each accomplishment that you would like to achieve by breaking it down into units of 4, 8 or 12 house chambers. The importance of doing this, is that you are giving what you want to achieve some type of rhythm.

Building the House
MT (Musical Tuning)

- **Determine and Document the goals for each house chamber**
    - The first chamber should be set as a manageable goal that is well within your means of accomplishing quickly.
    - Use the chart below to determine the goal of each chamber.
- **Set your environment. Everything around you physically, must agree with you.**
    - Pictures on your wall
    - Music you listen to
    - Use video story boards.
- **Process of Determination (what's going to emanate from you)**
    - Musical Tuning
    - Make sure people around you are in tune and in agreement with you.

- **Set your 12 Points of Significance – Minor Authentication**
  - These 12 points should be more related to or geared towards what you are trying to accomplish.

Energizing the House
ET (Electronic Tuning)

- **Set specific action towards what you are trying to accomplish.**
  - People must invest into you action oriented Attention.
  - People must invest into you action oriented Interest.
  - You must practice profitable relationships.
  - Eliminate diminished behavior towards you.
- **Look for Evidence**
  - Set your expectations.
  - Keep an eye out for components that meet your needs.
  - When something doesn't match up, disregard and look again.
  - Document your evidence.
- **Push your Energy Dynamics by determining your exchanges.**
  - Measure your exchanges.
  - After all exchanges you should have a sense of being on another level.
  - Exchange only with persons who have a consciousness of advancing you and your efforts.

Authenticate the House

- **Action Towards You – Major Authentication**
    - Investments
    - Integrity
    - Intimacy
        - Consciousness
        - Communication
        - Connection
        - Commitment
    - Increase
- **Your Consistent Action – Behavior Authentication**
    - Act towards your destiny daily.
    - Complete what you start.
    - Set these actions to be done within the first part of your day, every day.

Achieving Accomplishment

- **Take Measurement**
    - Make sure there is increase after each process.
    - Document your success; take pictures or video.
- **Mirror Into the Next House**
    - Exponential Push
    - Use the same strategies on all subsequent house chambers

1. Set Your Project

When setting your project into 4, 8 or 12 chambers, you are not setting them into to 4-12 equal parts, but 4-12 exponential parts. This is important because you are setting the stage for growth. You will use the accomplishment of the first chamber to create the basis for accomplishing the next. Work within one chamber at a time. Complete your first chamber first. Completing your first chamber sets the energy for all other chambers.

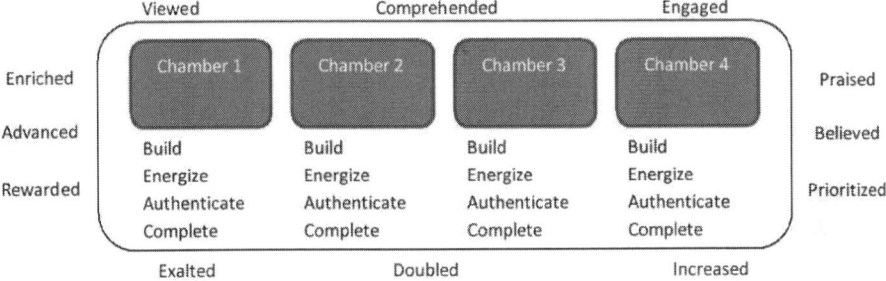

2. Set Your Relationships

You are also surrounding what you do with 12 points of significance. List below a person or persons that will deliver you a point of significance. A single individual can cover multiple points. Be sure to read the details of these points in the appendix, and make sure that the individuals are consistent with each point of significance.

Point	Person 1	Person 2	Person 3
Who Views You			
Who Comprehends You			
Who Engages You			
Who Praises You			
Who Believes in You			
Who Prioritizes You			
Who Enriches You			
Who Advances You			
Who Rewards You			
Who Exalts You			
Who Increases You			
Who Doubles You			

3. Infuse Previous Experience

Here you will take advantage of the past experiences of your own and the past experience of others to advance your projects. List the books, classes, seminars, names of mentors and advisors needed to give your project a foundation and that will also speed up your processes. Be sure to list your top 3 accomplishments, as you will need to have those at the forefront of your consciousness as you complete your task.

Points of Focus	1	2	3
Books			
Classes & Courses			
Seminars			
Mentors			
Advisors			
Past Accomplishments			

4. Set Your Timing

Use the charts below to determine what the goal of each chamber will be. Determine the overall goal of project A. For the most part, use whatever numerical value that is descriptive of your goal as your base number or your top cycle number – we will use a top sales goal in this example. Then use the charts below to help with your breakdown. Start with your top cycle number then multiply your top cycle number by the respective percentage to get a point of accomplishment for each chamber.

C1	C2	C3	C4
24%	38%	62%	100%

C1	C2	C3	C4	C5	C6	C7	C8
4%	6%	9%	15%	24%	38%	62%	100%

C1	C2	C3	C4	C5	C6	C7	C8	C9	C10	C11	C12
.3%	.5%	1%	2%	4%	6%	9%	15%	24%	38%	62%	100%

Here's a sample if you used the chart for 4 chambers with the top cycle being 1000 sales. There are many types of accomplishments; I am using sales in this example of sales because it covers a broader base of applications, but I will list other examples shortly.

Here when you set your task into 4 chambers, you have 4 cycles to complete.

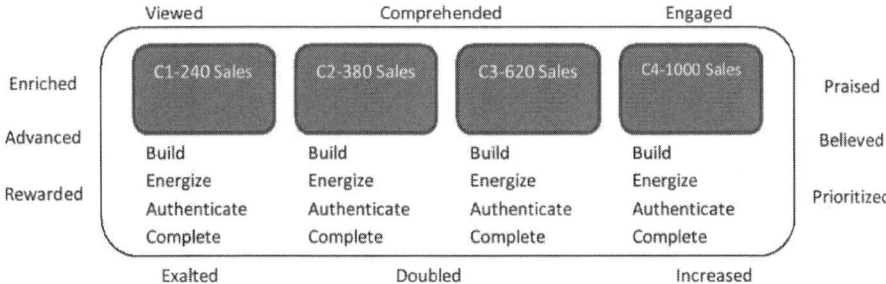

Here's a sample if you used the chart for 12 chambers with the top cycle being 1000 sales.

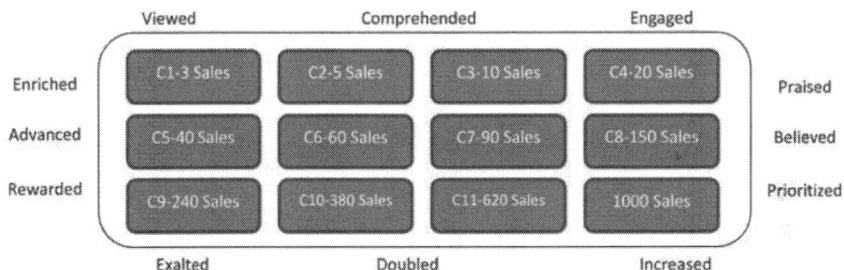

Notice I refer to each chamber as a cycle. When you set your tasks into 12 chambers, you have 12 cycles, where your first cycle is 3 sales or the equivalent in effort, and your last cycle is 1000 sales or the equivalent in effort for whatever factor is associated with what you want to accomplish. If there are no numbers associated with your task, be sure to break everything down in approximate value to the percentages given, always starting with a manageable and accomplishable first cycle or chamber 1.

Other Models of Accomplishment

Here are some other chamber types and cycles you can use to chart other numerical factors such as number of people, time, financial goals, or any other factor tied into what you would like to accomplish.

1. **Sales/Money Making Ventures**
   Use the same chart as the sales example and plug in the numbers.
   a. Starting a small business
   b. Increasing job related income goals
   c. Earning part-time or extra income using Network or Multi-Level marketing
   d. Getting out of debt

2. **Behavior Modification**
   You are not using numbers here, so insert into the first chamber a small manageable task and then put relative incremental task in the other chambers. Still start with knowing what your final task is before determining your first chamber. Your first chamber will be relatively smaller than your last chamber.
   a. Breaking bad habits
   b. Starting something new
   c. Improving job performance
   d. Organizing or reorganizing

3. **Building Relationships**
   Use the same chamber strategy as behavior modification.
   a. Improving marriage
   b. Building successful teams
   c. Finding love
   d. Increasing your network of supportive friends

4. **Health**
   Use a combination of strategies because some of these include numerical goals.
   a. Losing weight
   b. Setting an exercise regimen
   c. Eating better

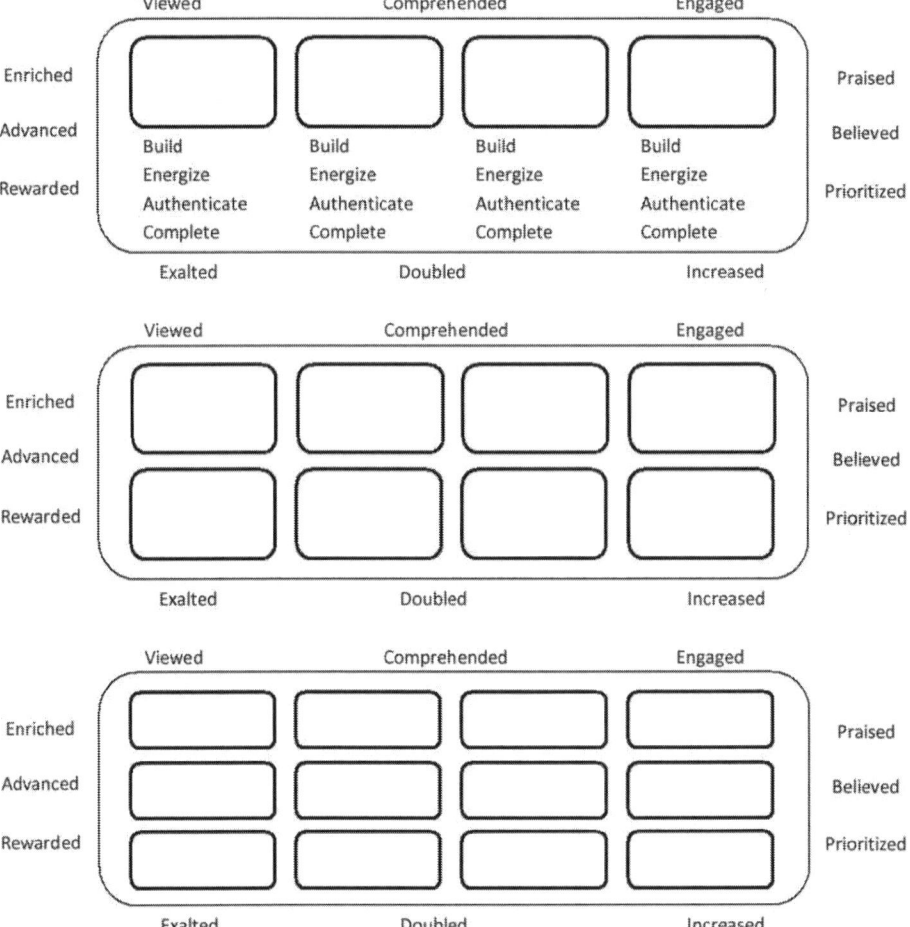

These are sample charts wherein you can insert your cycle values. I will include more in the appendix. I will also include more relationship forms.

Example 1 – Sales

If you goal is to open a bakery, but you don't have the financing or the ability to obtain financing. Plug into the last chamber what you picture yourself doing at your top cycle. Then ask yourself, "What can I afford to bake now?" If it's only 3 pies, put that in your first chamber cycle to bake 3 pies. In your second chamber cycle put in for example, 3 pies and 2 cakes and so on…Start. Completing your first chamber will make you just as successful as completing your last.

Example 2 – Behavior Modification

Let's say you want to stop smoking. Of course you will have zero cigarettes as your last cycle. So here you cut down smoking incrementally within each cycle. Start in your first chamber with a number down from what you are currently smoking. Make sure it's a reduction that you can handle. Here you would need to take full advantage of your 12 points of significance and your authentication processes, especially adding into the mix a Major Authenticator, someone that will help you to push time.

Example 3 – Building Relationships

Since relationships are about action towards persons, you have to take measurement of your actions given and measurement of the actions presented towards you. You put into your top cycle the desired goal for the relationship or relationships, both the number and/or type. Then you determine your actions in your first chamber cycle that are congruent with what you want to accomplish and build the house chambers incrementally.

Example 4 – Health

If you are losing weight, you can work the system like the sales model when it comes to setting up the cycles. If you are setting up an exercise regimen, set within the cycles your number of reps when comes to lifting weights, doing sit-ups or any other type of exercise regimen. Here again, use your authentications to propel you through your chambers.

In all of these, you set the first cycle, accomplish the first cycle, and then use it as a base to exponentially grow all other cycles. To do this, you repeat the first cycle by creating more energy and multiplying your efforts in the second cycle. This process ties you into natural cycles and seasons that have been in existence since the beginning of time and is also imbedded in both chemical and biological systems.

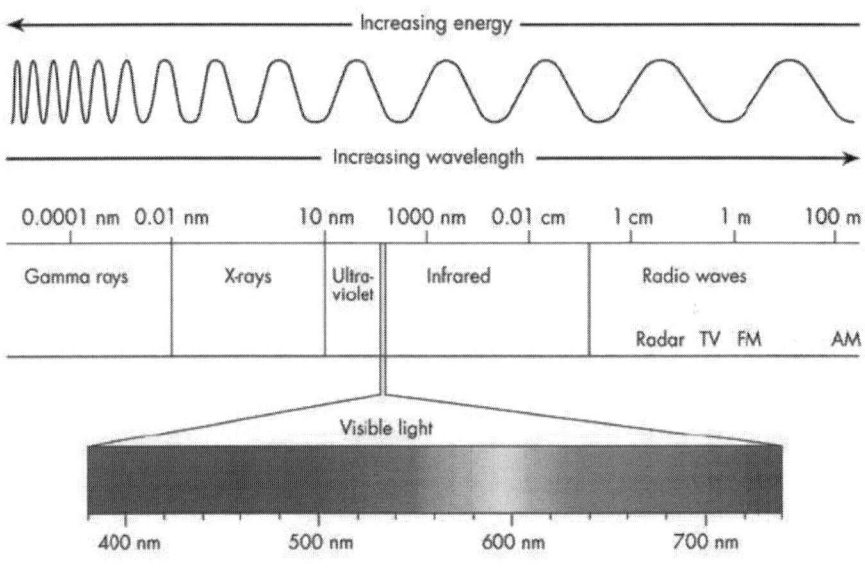

Everything on earth cycles, and has more cycles built within.

The Music of the Mind Field

Implementing this chapter in your daily routine will enhance your ability to create the life that you want. Most people can think without limitation, but most people cannot create without limitation. To help you with this, I would like to the words assign some values to "thinking" and "creating".

Thinking	*Creating*
Mental	Physical
Spirit	Body
Heaven	Earth

What we see here on earth are the particles of images within the whole of everything reflected into existence in which we can presently experience. What we create, we experience, and what we create comes from what we think.

Creating	*Thinking*
Physical	Mental
Body	Spirit
Earth	Heaven

So in retrospect,

the Physical comes from the Mental,
the Body comes from the Spirit,
the Earth comes from Heaven,
and Creations come from the Mind.

Thinking	*Creating*
Mental	Physical
Spirit	Body
Heaven	Earth
Mind	**Creations**

Mind Field

But the one thing I want to focus on here, is how do your personal creations become limited? How can you move from being limited to being unlimited?

Can it be that unlimited minds produce unlimited creations, and limited minds produce limited creations? Sounds simple enough. But, maybe not.

Let's look closely at a major fact. Anything you see created outside of nature is a product of someone's mind. The pencil that you write with came from someone's mind. The computer that you work and play on came from someone's mind. The cell phone that you talk on came from someone's mind. The store that you shop in came from someone's mind. The clothes that you wear came from someone's mind. You get the picture? All of life is imaged from the mind.

I was asked a very tough question at one of my seminars, "Where do all the great ideas and inventions come from? How do these great things and ideas get assigned to some people and not others?"

My answer to them was that everyone on earth is equally rich in their ability to access greatness, but not everyone equally accesses their greatness. You yourself are a production of an initial image just like a cell phone, clothes, or a pencil. Everything starts with an image, and the physical result is a reflection of that image. So what you want to accomplish doesn't need to be made, but reflected.

Before an architect builds a house, there is an image. Before your mother fixes your breakfast, there is an image. Before your cell phone made it to the store shelf, there was an image. You yourself was an image before you came into existence as the reflection of that same image. No one is born with any greater image than the other, so we all have the same opportunity to reflect unlimited greatness.

What you want to accomplish doesn't need to be made, but reflected.

Thinking	*Creating*
Mental	Physical
Spirit	Body
Heaven	Earth
Mind	**Creations**
Image	**Reflection**

As I said earlier, most people can think without limitation, but most people cannot create without limitation. This is due to the fact that one can harbor reflection issues as well as image issues. If you can get a correct view of your personal image, then you can properly connect to your reflection. Within this, nothing becomes impossible. This is why it is important to dismiss shame and learn your true value. Everything you want to accomplish, when accomplished is just a reflection. A reflection of what? You. You cannot see your accomplishment without seeing you. So, I will start by helping you with the word "image". But first, I must add two more values to the chart - 1 & 8. I'll explain later what 1 and 8 is.

Thinking	*Creating*
Mental	Physical
Spirit	Body
Heaven	Earth
Mind	**Creations**
Image	**Reflection**
1	8

The process between Thinking and Creating, the Mental and the Physical, Dreaming of the Life You Want To Accomplish and Creating the Life You Want is not a 1-2 process, but a 1 through 8 process. Let's go back to the word image.

Image
Imagine

Imagination is the key. Anyone can imagine anything and anyone can imagine everything. Imagination is a unique world which is completely separated from any physical condition. Imagination is anyone's opportunity to press pass any undesired condition, but not everyone has the same capability to reflect their imagination into reality for experience. So, I would like to break down the word Imagine for you in a very unique and credible way in order for you to gain the ability to create without limits.

Ima/gine

The suffix of the word imagine comes from the Old English -ginari, gin, or go. I want you to look at a similar word to further expand the use of the word "Imagine" and use a word that contains the same suffix - Engine. Here we can further break down the suffix -gine. The suffix -gine derives from the old French -gin and the Latin -genium which is related to the Latin suffix -genious. Tied in with its original form -kin, you come up with this expansive definition: **the ability to produce and to convert energy into useful mechanical motion.** This leads me to believe that all imagination is meant to be produced for experience.

Now I don't want you to miss the Latin suffix -genium or -genious, which means to possess the high intelligence to produce after one's imagination. So "imagine" can be broken up as follows:

Ima/genius

So here's where I'm going with this

Imagine
I'm a/genius

The Music of the Mind Field

If you can imagine it, you have to go after your genius to produce it. You cannot separate production from imagination. So imagination is not just relegated to what you can bring to your mind, but imagination is your ability to take what's on your mind and produce "like kind" outside of your mind. Like kind, -kin, -gen or to generate or birth something into existence. This is what genius is all about. You cannot think of something great and then dismiss it! Everyone is a genius. Everyone is a producer.

So again, the process of "genius" is an eight-step process and not a two-step process. Anybody can be a genius and create the life that they want and desire.

Here is The Master Key System to genius:

Key #1
"...Unity, Beginning, Desire, To Begin, To Start, Initial Source, One-ness, Light, Initial Energy Source, Original Image, First, To Be First..."

Key #2
"...Unfolding, To Unfold, First of the Physical, Context, To Bring Into Context, Initial Balance, Yin & Yang, Divide Into Sections, Mental Groundwork, Planting, Documenting Evidence, Organization..."

Key #3
"...Beginning of Growth, Mental Growth, Multiplication, Maturity, Veiw-Point of Perfection, Information That Leads To Formation, Intimacy, Germination, Synergy ..."

Key #4
"...Formation, Completion, Acquiring What's Next, Creation, Material Development, Accessing Supply, Consummation, Making Your Move..."

Key #5
"...Mental Clarity, Grace, Spirit, Information of Inspiration, Inspiration, Your "Ah ha" Moment, Revelation, To See Clearly..."

Key #6
"...Labor, What It Takes To Get The Job Done, Personal Effort, Personal Investment of Active Time, Your Active Contribution..."

Key #7
"...Perfection, Experiencing What Is True, Rest, Enjoying What Is Produced Completion, Ecstasy, Bliss..."

Key #8
"...Resurrection, Regeneration, Reflection, Back To Unity, Back To One, Mirroring The Source, Living Your Beginning, Become Your Beginning, Memory..."

These keys are also steps. The 8 steps are for everyone and not just the Bill Gates, Steve Jobs, Oprah Winfreys and Sam Waltons of the world. Do not dismiss your own genius, thusly dismissing your greatness.

Here's how it works.

It's all about imaging and imagination. But this goes a few steps beyond visualizing, although visualizing is an important component of imaging. By the time you see a product that is manifested into existence, what you actually see is a regeneration of something that was already in existence in someone's mind. Everything is a regeneration of something and things always regenerate off of an image. Photographers readily accept this whole concept, because they work with images that actually exist in two to three places simultaneously. The reflections are actually what is being generated from the image.

Now I know a good number of people reading this book are not musicians, but for you to understand fully how to bring your desires into existence, I must turn you into a music student, and for good reason. Let me remind you of our word association in which we will now turn into a number association.

Thinking	*Creating*
Mental	Physical
Spirit	Body
Heaven	Earth
Mind	**Creations**
Image	**Reflection**
1	**8**

The Music of the Mind Field

We will use a scale on the piano to paint a very accurate picture of how this works.

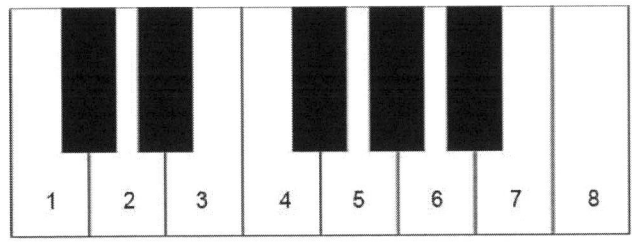

On the piano, 1 and 8 are the same note. 8 sonically is just a higher pitch, but it is exactly the same note as 1. It's just like counting the days of the week from Sunday to Sunday. Sunday is the 1st day of the week, but the next Sunday can be considered the 1st day of the next week or the 8th day from the last Sunday. Now as you go up the scale the values on the chart alternate. Here is an example.

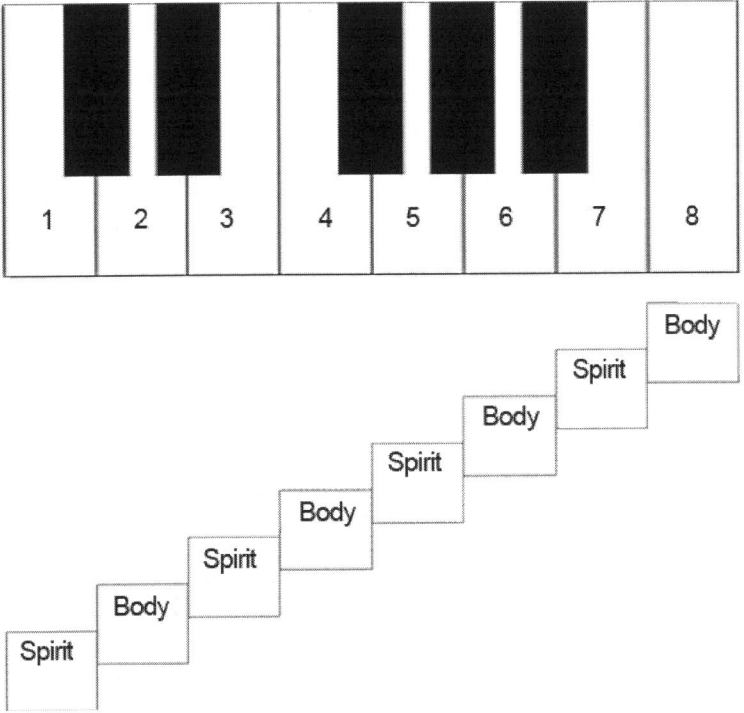

Based on this scale you should notice that the Spirit and Body, or the Mental and the Physical (1 and 8) are actually the same. 8 is the regeneration of 1. But to properly regenerate 8, you must go through the process of 2-7 in which we miss most of the time. Here, you have to use The Master Key System provided to get a general idea of what needs to happen from steps 1-8. You can then associate these with the Thinking and Creating diagram.

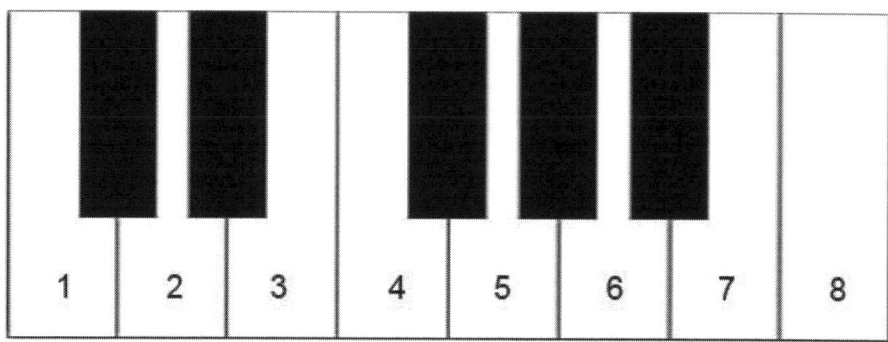

Thinking	Creating	Thinking	Creating	Thinking	Creating	Thinking	Creating
Mental	Physical	Mental	Physical	Mental	Physical	Mental	**Physical**
Spirit	Body	Spirit	Body	Spirit	Body	Spirit	**Body**
Heaven	Earth	Heaven	Earth	Heaven	Earth	Heaven	**Earth**
Mind	Creation	Mind	Creation	Mind	Creation	Mind	**Creation**
Image	Reflection	Image	Reflection	Image	Reflection	Image	**Reflection**
1	2	3	4	5	6	7	**8**

As you alternate your personal process from Thinking and Creating, assign the appropriate Master Key to mirror the behavior associated with the step.

The Music of the Mind Field

Key #1 - *Thinking, Mental, Spirit, Heaven, Mind, Image*

"...Unity, Beginning, Desire, To Begin, To Start, Initial Source, Oneness, Light, Initial Energy Source, Original Image, First, To Be First..."

Key #2 - *Creating, Physical, Body, Earth, Creation, Reflection*

"...Unfolding, To Unfold, First of the Physical, Context, To Bring Into Context, Initial Balance, Yin & Yang, Divide Into Sections, Mental Groundwork, Planting, Documenting Evidence, Organization..."

Key #3 - *Thinking, Mental, Spirit, Heaven, Mind, Image*

"...Beginning of Growth, Mental Growth, Multiplication, Maturity, Veiw-Point of Perfection, Information That Leads To Formation, Intimacy, Germination, Synergy ..."

Key #4 - *Creating, Physical, Body, Earth, Creation, Reflection*

"...Formation, Completion, Acquiring What's Next, Creation, Material Development, Accessing Supply, Consummation, Making Your Move..."

Key #5 - *Thinking, Mental, Spirit, Heaven, Mind, Image*

"...Mental Clarity, Grace, Spirit, Information of Inspiration, Inspiration, Your "Ah ha" Moment, Revelation, To See Clearly..."

Key #6 - *Creating, Physical, Body, Earth, Creation, Reflection*

"...Labor, What It Takes To Get The Job Done, Personal Effort, Personal Investment of Active Time, Your Active Contribution..."

Key #7 - *Thinking, Mental, Spirit, Heaven, Mind, Image*

"...Perfection, Experiencing What Is True, Rest, Enjoying What Is Produced Completion, Ecstasy, Bliss..."

Key #8

"...Resurrection, Regeneration, Reflection, Back To Unity, Back To One, Mirroring The Source, Living Your Beginning, Become Your Beginning, Memory..."

By the time you reach #8, #8 should be the exact physical manifestation of what you had on your mind, which is #1. Again, you would have created the physical component of your mental component. Or better stated, you have generated or regenerated what already existed in your mind. To imagine is to also generate. All of life is about generation. Everyone on earth is connected to the Whole of Everything and is capable of generating anything that comes to mind, and everyone on earth has the gift of genius. You too can connect to your reflection.

But start here, with proper imaging.

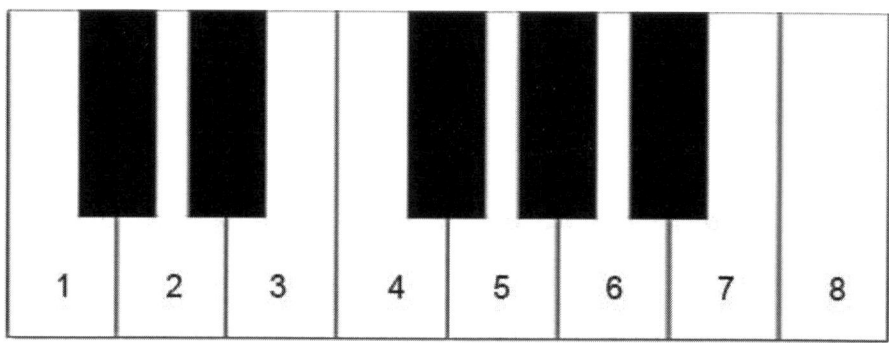

2-4-6-8 is about Connecting.

1-3-5-7 is about Reflecting.

Going back to the breakdown of the word imaging we discover the following works well as an exercise.

Imagine
I'm a/genius

The Music of the Mind Field

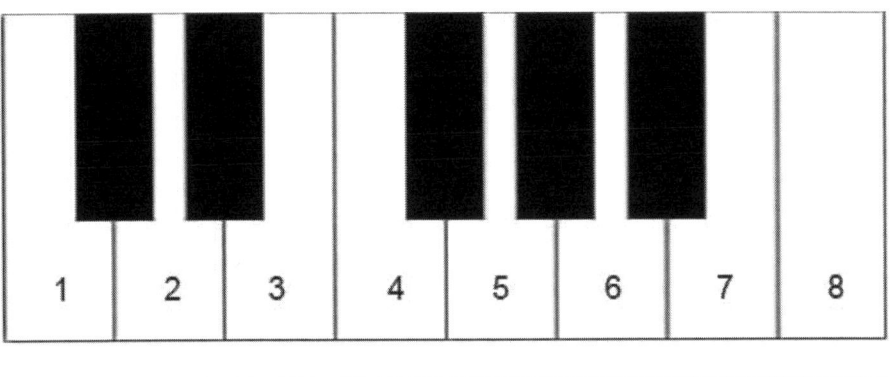

| I Am | Genius | I Am | Genius | I Am | Genius | I Am | Genius |

Imagine

Thinking	Creating	Thinking	Creating	Thinking	Creating	Thinking	Creating
Mental	Physical	Mental	Physical	Mental	Physical	Mental	**Physical**
Spirit	Body	Spirit	Body	Spirit	Body	Spirit	**Body**
Heaven	Earth	Heaven	Earth	Heaven	Earth	Heaven	**Earth**
Mind	Creation	Mind	Creation	Mind	Creation	Mind	**Creation**
Image	Reflection	Image	Reflection	Image	Reflection	Image	**Reflection**
1	2	3	4	5	6	7	**8**
Reflect	Connect	Reflect	Connect	Reflect	Connect	Reflect	**Connect**

| I Am | Genius | I Am | Genius | I Am | Genius | I Am | Genius |

"I Am" is your point of discovery. "Genius" is your point of creating more of who you are. So set this cadence for your life and practice:

1 "I Am"   2 "A Genius"
3 "I Am"   4 "A Genius"
5 "I Am"   6 "A Genius"
7 "I Am"   8 "A Genius"

1 "Reflect"   2 "Connect"
3 "Reflect"   4 "Connect"
5 "Reflect"   6 "Connect"
7 "Reflect"   8 "Connect"

Mind Field

1 "Think"   2 "Create"
3 "Think"   4 "Create"
5 "Think"   6 "Create"
7 "Think"   8 "Create"

Every time you create something, you are a genius. You connect to your reflection. But the greater point here is that you do have a reflection, you do have an image, you do have a mind to create unlimited images into reality, and now you have the blue print to create an unlimited life!

The Science of the Mind Field

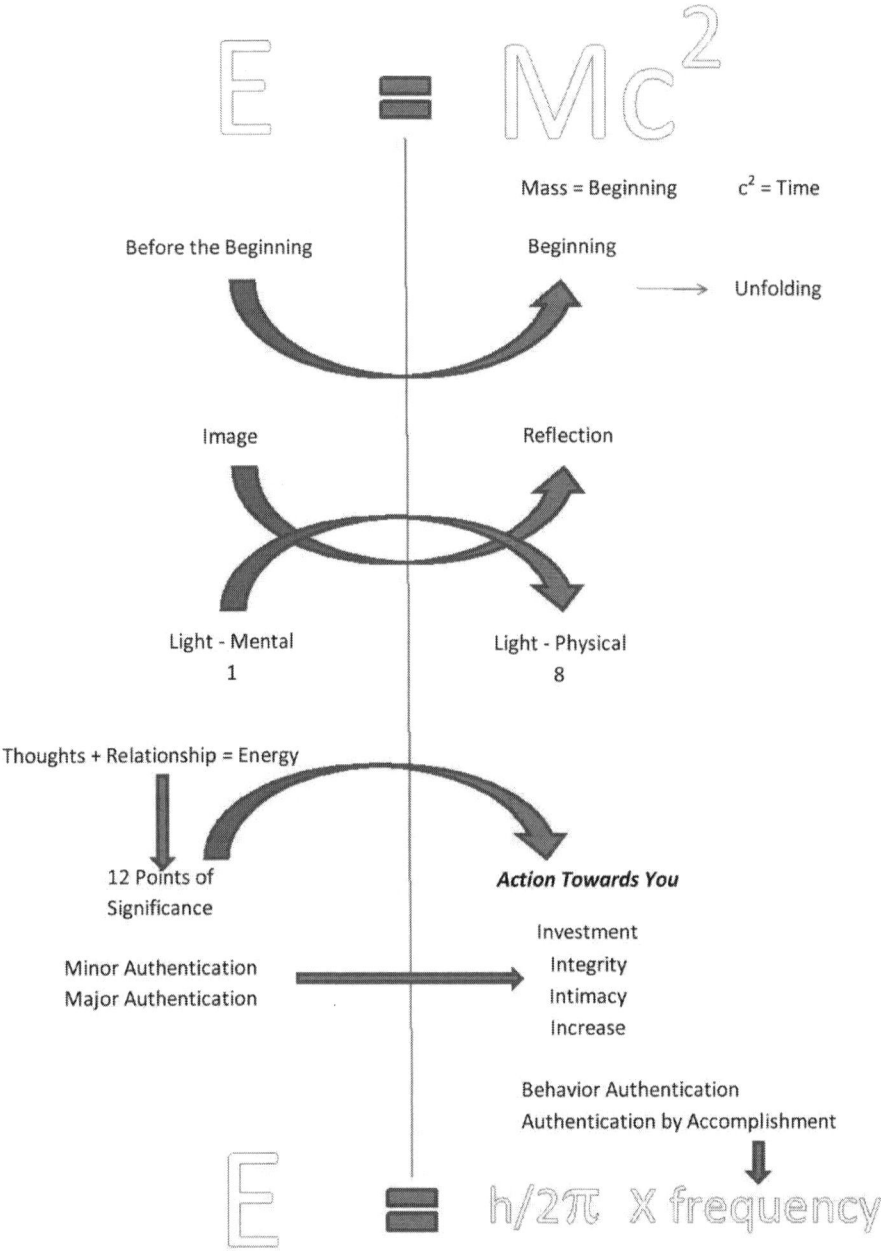

Mind Field

Here is the process of accomplishment in scientific terms:

1. **Set the Formula**
2. **Set the Energy**
3. **Set the Frequency**
4. **Recognize your Constants**

Every beginning has a "before the beginning", and it is what you do "before the beginning" that is the key to life and accomplishment. I know a good number of people are not scientific by nature, but don't let the previous chart scare you. I will give you as clear of a breakdown as possible. I'm not using these formulas for Energy as a scientific formula, but as a model for accomplishment and for you to see the parallels as to how energy works in much the same way for all of life and not just science. As you understand these formulas to be a proven law as it concerns energy, your ability to accomplish whatever you want in life also becomes a law as you set the energy for what you want.

If you can begin to understand that your success is a law, you will then be able to put that law to work for you. Most people don't know that they need to live their life "before the beginning" instead of living as a responsive entity "after the beginning" once things are already set. It is here that not a lot of thought is given. Most primarily live consciously in the physical, and then unconsciously in the mental or spiritual. If you learn to live consciously in the mental and the spiritual, then you don't have to be as conscious of the physical, because things work out without fail automatically.

What I am saying here is, live on the side where energy is created, and that is "before the beginning". It all starts with energy, and we can use energy as an entry-point into the scientific portion of the Mind Field.

So let's take a quick look at the elements of both formulas. I will be drawing on the principal of each formula as a model for success.

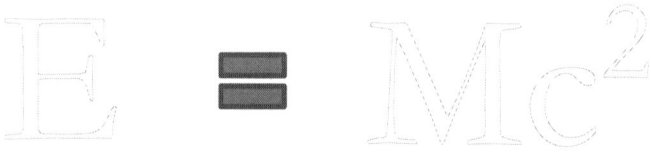

Of course we know here that (E) represents Energy. (M) represents physical mass, and (c^2) is a constant which is the speed of light. (c^2) is a representation of the measurement of time and what can be accomplished in time, and then how time can be consistent towards delivering results.

So let's make the first associations to success by using this formula.

Results happen in the physical, but you need Energy to create results. You set the energy by determining your design and setting your relationships to that design which all happens "before the beginning". The beginning starts at the first sign of physical evidence that represents what you are trying to accomplish, but there is a "before the beginning" in which you must become conscious of.

1. Set the Formula

Determine an endpoint to your Design. Never keep your ideas and wants open-ended. Terminate what doesn't work for you. (Setting the formula)

The word Determination and the word Definition are related word concepts. The root word of determine is "termine" which means to terminate. The root word for define is finite, which is the same as making things final or bringing things to an end. How is this important to your personal development?

Once you have a design established, that design must have an end-point established in your mind so you can have a beginning point to work with outside of your mind. This end-point established in your mind is "before the beginning". Every flight of a commercial airliner has a flight plan and a determined destination for landing. What if you booked a flight that was open-ended? It would never work. It's quite simple, finishing something is important. Reaching a destination is vital once you start the journey.

Determination is the process of placing final points to your design. You need these final points not just for yourself, but you need them for others who might play a role in getting you to your destination. Have you ever thought for a little, why airport terminals are called terminals? Termination is related to your destination. Everyone from the flight crew, to the ground crew, to air traffic control all have the same determination to coordinate a flight, and guiding the flight to its destination. This is vital, because with anyone of these entities being off by any measure, this can spell disaster for the traveler.

Agreement

The same holds true for the design in your mind based off of your desire. It was discussed earlier the importance of the "Mind". Everything you see in existence outside of nature started in someone's mind or "before the beginning". With this being a fact, one might conclude that the mind is the most vital component of human existence. But there is one component of human existence that stands even greater than the human mind. That component is agreement. Without agreement nothing within the mind can function outside of the mind. Agreement is the single most important word in human history. Here's where the word termination or determination becomes vital to the process of your personal success.

Everything in existence has at its base, Energy, as we see in Albert Einstein's formula. If it contains protons, neutrons, and electrons, it is governed by energy. To determine what something is going to be, you must set its energy. Energy is measured in hertz, and every animate and inanimate object can be measured in hertz. Hertz is quite frequently referred to as frequency or wave patterns, and how frequencies interact determines what a substance is. To simplify what frequencies are, we can define them as wave patterns or rhythms. So any substances that exist are simply a complex interaction of rhythms. So to determine what a "thing" is to be, you must pin point a basis to establish the energy needed to bring some "thing" into reality or a finite point. So let's look at the second formula for Energy:

Here (h/2π) represents two known constants - (h) represents a physical constant and (2π) is a mathematical constant. The purpose of mentioning these constants is to engrain in your thinking and your mind that there are laws that are constants working on your behalf!

It is within these constants that we all are equally rich. (h), which is a physical constant and (2π) which is a mathematical constant works on behalf of everybody in the world the exact same way, the same goes for (c^2) and the speed of light which is also a constant. The only difference between any substance is the amount of energy and the rate of energy. The only difference between somebody who is extremely successful and someone who is failing is how their personal energy is placed. The way you determine the rate of Energy is how you treat frequency.

2. Set the Energy

Set the energy by determining your agreements. (Energy)

The mind can define and design based on a desire, but it cannot set energy. It can't do it, period. Energy is set by agreement. Agreement is a determination on how things work together in order for other things to exist. This is why people "make plans" and "set goals" all day long, but never do anything. There is no energy. But here's that word again. Determination. Why?

To determine what something is going to be, you must set its energy.

What's fundamental to agreement is termination. This concept might seem strange, but it's how things are. We actually make determinations by the process of elimination.

What?

Mind Field

The Process of Elimination By Termination

You are in a constant state of relationship. You are in a constant state of exchange. You are in a constant state of becoming one. All of these are true by default and are represented by these same mathematical and scientific constants. Everything on earth, in order for it to exist has to be in relationship to something. Even the breath that you breathe is a relationship. If it didn't work right, you would cease to exist. Relationships always foster energy in one form or the other, and one of the best examples of this is photosynthesis. All organisms require energy for their chemical reactions. These reactions may be involved with reproduction, growth, and other activities.

Every cell in your body is in a constant state of relationship. It is the nature of these relationships that form the basis of life and existence. What happens when one component of a stated relationship ceases to cooperate? Dysfunction would set in and the organism, whatever it may be, will begin to move towards decay and eventually death. This is true for a microorganism such as a simple cell structure and a macro-organism such as an airport, corporation, or even a government.

Organisms found in nature and in your body have set contingencies for just this matter. Whenever any part of the whole ceases to function, it is terminated. This must be so, or the whole organism will follow the direction of the dysfunctional part into decay and death. Even in the organism called a corporation, when an employee is of no use to the goal of the whole, he or she is dismissed. If it is determined that a pilot is not competent to get you to your destination, it is prudent that action is taken and that pilot is terminated from the process.

May I state a fact that is not readily recognized?

Thank you.

Every human on earth, being in a constant state of relationship is also always in a full state of interactivity at all times. Again, this is a constant just like the speed of light and gravity. What I mean by this, is that every human on earth is fully connected. This is a part of your complete existence, being fully connected at all times. The question then is not of the connectivity, but whom and what one is connected to. Connection determines energy and energy determines state. The constant is our status and the variable is our state.

Connection determines energy and energy determines state.

If something bad or less desirable happens to a person, it is not because they are missing a connection; it is because they are connected to some source that creates that situation. Again, it is important to realize that at all times you are fully connected. If something bad happens, that "bad" has a source, and at some point and time, you came into agreement with that source that created the energy field for that very situation to come into existence.

You are in a constant state of agreement with something and someone at all times. The status of connection never changes, only the type of connection changes, and then the resulting energy changes with it.

Agreement sets energy, and only through two or more sources working in proximity can energy be produced. Why is this important? Just like in nature, science, and even within a successful corporation you have to become proficient at terminating things that don't work. A relationship to something or someone who doesn't agree with your destination will always produce bad results. Why? Because a relationship of any kind is still an agreement, and agreements set the energy that facilitates form, whether that form ends up being good for you or bad for you.

Sometimes we stick with bad agreements and then try to work them out. That's why I tell people don't try to solve problems, because solving an issue brings you into a relationship to that issue, which then creates the problem. This will change your energy based on the scientific formulas we are reviewing.

The key here is to see more than what you might consider to be the problem that is registering in your presence. More always exist, because you always have access to "before the beginning". If something bad presents itself, there is definitely something that's in disagreement with your design. Something or someone is out of line with your appointments. Signs on your roadmap are being disregarded. Whatever it is, once identified, it must be terminated. This is how real and true determinations are made. Don't become a problem solver, become an idea generator.

Don't become a problem solver, become an idea generator.

Remember here, we are simply directing the energy into what is to be formed to reach a specific destination. It is here that we make our adjustments, and to make sure that everything stay in alignment with our stated goals. When you change the energy, you redirect the destiny. If the person fueling a plane headed to California from Florida misses his cue based on assigned directives, that flight would be cut short of its destination because the line of wrong energy was not addressed and terminated.

After creation is completed in the mind and the design is set based on that creation, relationships are then fostered to address the creation that promotes those initial energy streams that eventually bring the form of that design into reality. When you have a point of destination set and a non-profitable agreement has pulled you off course, you have to terminate the wrong direction, thusly setting you back on the right path.

When you change the energy, you redirect the destiny.

3. Set the Frequency

Set your patterns of behavior and then set the patterns of behavior towards you. (Frequency)

Here's a clearer example. When somebody disappoints you, they actually didn't. You put yourself in a line of agreement with that person, which then led to the disappointment. So what you must do is terminate that direction, because no matter how much you try to push, your destination will never be reached. It's important to note here that all the responsibility falls on you, because you are the master designer. You can require another person to make an adjustment to accommodate your dream, but if they can't make the adjustment, you must make the termination, which then becomes your determination.

The soul of determination is about making cuts and letting go. It's about terminating people, places, and things that do not line up with the efforts of your destination and putting aside what doesn't work for you. It's about setting your 12 points of Significance and your Authentications, which affects your frequency.

4. Recognize your Constants

Look for evidence and then relate to your evidence. (Constants)

Evidence in this case becomes your constant. It is the proof that you are on the right track and you are fostering the right relationships that are related to your dream and destiny. Let's look at the first constant in the formulas:

(C^2) is the speed of light. Light and time works the same for everyone. The key here is that there is one thing that travels faster than the speed of light, and that's the speed of your thoughts. Behind every thought energy is created. The energy that is created from a thought extends out into the universe, and is never left out there randomly to sit in the air or in the ether doing nothing. It is an actual energy that has its own frequency and quality. So consider your thoughts as a musical notes or a sound waves.

Just like a radio signal, your thoughts are being picked up by someone and something at all times. This is why I stated that you are in a constant status of relationships at all times. So the timing of your thoughts being reached and received is done in an instant as it is ruled by (c^2). So because substance exist (Mass), substance is instantly interrelated to your thoughts at the speed of light.

All that has to happen at this point is you becoming conscious of what's available for you to arrange into your destiny. Here again, you set your energy so that it is in place for you to realize what's available to you as it comes across your path physically. It could be a person. It could be a special circumstance. It could be things. It could be in the form of an opportunity. This is the same law of energy that is in affect when you use your cell phone, pick up on an internet 4G signal, or tune your cable's converter box to get a specific channel. If you are not tuned into your line of substance, you will miss it. So take the time to review the chapter on Callings and focus on the section on tuning.

The next constant (h) is called Plank's constant, which is a physical constant. Although Plank's constant refers to the measurement of particles and waves on an atomic level, the principles are the same when it comes to moving your ideas, dreams, and desires from your mind into the physical. The dimension of Planck's constant is the product of energy multiplied by time, a quantity called action. Not to get too detailed, I'll move on and make the point. The formula which involves (h) and (π) deals with the spin of an electron around its orbit in time.

So you want to set the time for what you want to accomplish into a cycle and a season. So again, let's look at a simple cycle for a house chamber.

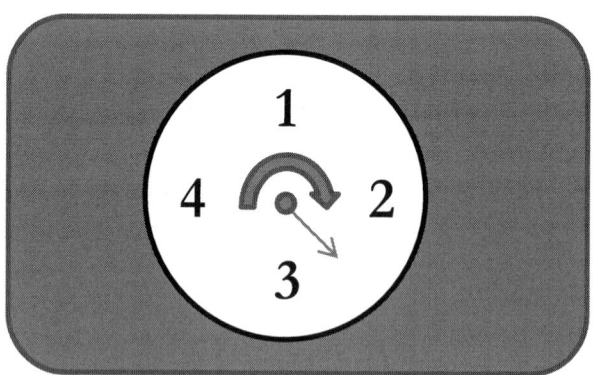

1. Build the house.
2. Energize the house.
3. Authenticate the house.
4. Achieving Accomplishment.

This sets a cycle and a rhythm. Then you must put that rhythm into a time cycle. Once this is done within your first chamber you will have a better idea as to what your season is. Now as you move on to your second chamber, you can multiply your efforts by increasing the energy and the 4 levels of authentication. This will push the time of the second house. It will shorten the cycle, and increase your results exponentially.

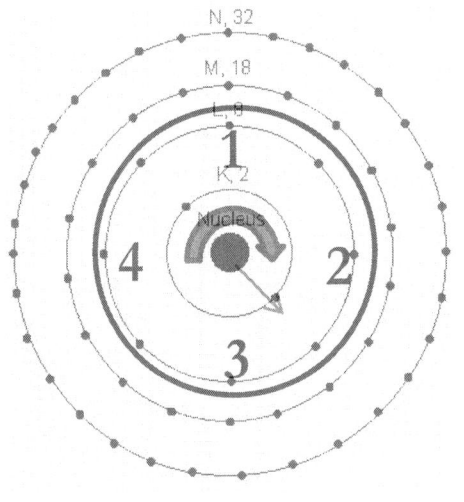

The electron spinning around the nucleus of an atom works and cycles on the same basis.

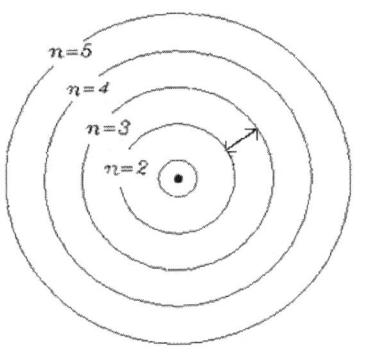

Beyond the nucleus, the electron orbits grow exponentially, and as they grow the more energy is contained.

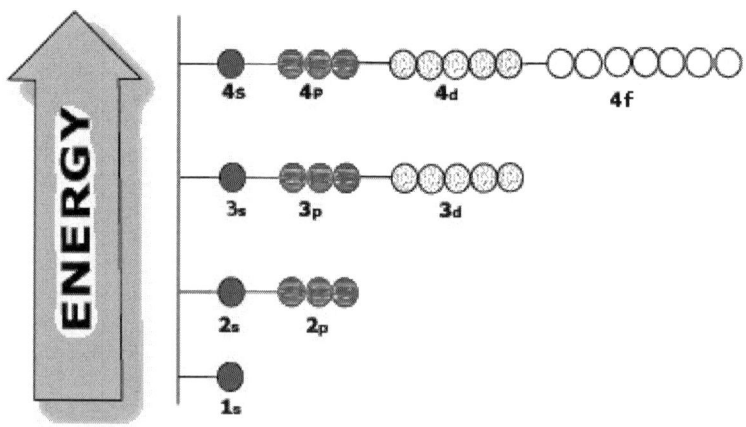

The point is when the constants are multiplied by frequency, it determines energy. So the type frequency invested in your project determines what substances show up and how your physical substances behave. Frequencies based on the timing of people's behavior towards you, and it is also a matter of your own personal commitment and behavior towards what you want to accomplish. Remember, matter is only a solidified form of light.

So your evidence is determined by your frequency. When you can't see the evidence that supports what you want in life, go back and remake the determinations in your authentications and look again. You do not have to accept anything as it is in front of you, if it's not right – look again. Once you have the components of your evidence aligned, arrange your melody and you will see results. This is the Mind Field and your keys to accomplishment.

The Spirit of the Mind Field

What is very interesting is how religious beliefs, especially within the Western society, have affected how we view the mind and spirituality. I want to note here, that not all religious people are successful. It would seem that since we are dealing with religion and God, that more people would be successful in life. So what is it that we believe that keeps a good number of people in a perpetual struggle from day-to-day even though people go to church weekly?

This chapter is not a challenge to the religious norms of within today's society, but I want to use some of our current religious beliefs as a backdrop to the Mind Field in order to bring a greater understanding as to how the Mind Field works.

The "You" That Exist Beyond "You"
What Scares Today's Christian

There seems to be this insatiable need to be low, feel low, and to be undervalued. Feeling low for the most part is a safety mechanism for those who can't explain life or figure out a way to escape their failures in life. Primarily, the thought is, is that if you start with a low mind-set, complete with the corresponding feelings, you can successfully deal with life's disappointments and life's failures can then become manageable.

Many people live well below their God given potential, and sometimes today's religions set the environment for this type of lackluster living. A good number of people miss the fact that they are way more than they think they are and give themselves credit to be. What in the world do I mean by this?

Human potential is unlimited, but a lot of people have found a way to live with limitations. As human beings, we are way more than we give ourselves credit to be. We have hidden our greatest selves in a dark closet because of the fear of loss and the fear of death. Most people are fighting to protect and to preserve the puniest life existence. This is because they live with the mindset that all that they have in life is their immediate surroundings in which most count to be insufficient. So people fight to protect the little that they have.

Protecting the little and preserving the little is all done at the expense of our greater selves.

For the most part, today's major religious institutions play a major role in authenticating the smallness and shortness of this little life that we are "privileged with", so we do everything we can not to lose it. There seems to be this big God, and then there is the little people on earth who are left with the only option of making sure this big God stays pleased. This creates an existence of survival, and for the most part, a great number of people miss the opportunity to live great lives when this is their engrained focus. Energy is sapped up trying to be like this big God in order to win His approval, or more importantly, trying to be "good" for God. We don't want to mess up or God will exact "loss" upon our lives. This is the basic tenant of most religious settings.

What is missed here is, being made in the image of God seems to tell me that you are who He is. Yes, equal to God! But how afraid are most religions of that?

Religious Ideas versus The Mind

Most people believe in a higher power and this higher power has many references. It all depends on what religious persuasion you come from or what belief system you hold that determines what and who this higher power is. Most of today's protestant churches claim to have a lock on the doings and movements of this great God. But somehow a great God automatically denotes that His subjects, the people on earth, are less than who God is by default. "Don't dare to express yourself as being higher than the definition God has imposed on you! That is blasphemous!", some would say.

So people start with the ideology that there is this big old God who made us little, itty-bitty humans, and we ought to stay in our place. This forces an imprisoning mindset of being "less than".

The Spirit of the Mind Field

This is a dangerous equation!

May I submit to you here that we grossly misunderstand the phrase "let Us make man in Our image" found in the book of Genesis in the Christian Bible. There are two key words here, and we subconsciously use one word to cancel out the other. We tend to focus on the supposed fact that we were "made", but the word "image" conflicts with the word "made". Can you actually make an image? No. An image is subject to the fact that something already exists in order for there to be an image. So if we think we are "made", then we must think of ourselves as less than our maker. But if we are an actual image or a reflection of something, then our image is "made" by what is already in existence becoming visible. You might not get this in a traditional religion.

So "made", in this case, doesn't denote being made from scratch, but simply becoming a visible form of what is already in existence. So the idea here is that you are the visible form of who God is. What is actually made is a reflection. It is important here at this point to understand that there is an existence that exists in fullness, and anything that is "made" is not actually "made", but reflected.

"What in the hell...!!!???", you might ask.

Most of today's religions, especially in the West would reject this notion; thinking, aren't we so messed up, so evil, we can't get things right, we make mistakes, get sick, cheat, lie, steal...? How can this be? Are we not "less than" because of these things? If truly, at one time we were like God, didn't Adam and Eve mess that up for all of us?

Man, that's some real power. Can one woman eat a piece of fruit and mess up the whole human race?!?? If so, then this one act becomes the most powerful act ever! This would then make Eve superhuman, having the power to screw up all of mankind. And so we believe. And poor us. Poor struggling mankind. Waahh, Waahh, Waahh! Now we need a Religious Baby Bottle so we can at least get a sensation that we are all ok.

We are like an infant, needing God to "feed" us because we deem ourselves as helpless humans and God will cater to our needs if we are good enough or "favored". This completely knocks out the truth that we are who He is and replaces it with the ideal that God messed up by making a faulty existence called the Human Being, and we are all included in this major global experiment that went awry. Now because of this human error that God made, we need to meet every week to pay homage to this big God, learn to do right, or get zapped. Somehow this seems to make people comfortable. That's what we need, comfort; and this religious baby bottle seems to do the trick. In a lot of cases, people's lives do not seem to improve while they are comforted by their religious beliefs.

It is said "Stop crying about life. God's going to "fix" it. By the way leave me a check before you leave church". Some are very afraid to ask the question, "Does my religious beliefs improve my life, or do I hang on to the supposed fact that one day God will make it better, even if it means dying first and getting my reward in heaven at a later time?" Is this really who God is?

Most people are comfortable with the idea of being less than who God is. Less than the Universal Intelligence. Less than our true beginnings. Less than who we are called to be. Less than our true image. Less than our true potency. People become religious about their self-imposed limitations and look for religious satisfaction to validate their imposed lowliness along with comfortable catch phrases such as, "God - nobody is greater than you", and "Only God is worthy", and within this, people lose their own self-worth. Somehow it is believed that in making ourselves "less than", we appease this big God, and then from that point we are then loved.

You can readily see how this causes an expansive and explosive psychosis. This is how a good number of people deal with the world around them. Be "less than" so you can win approval and thusly be loved. But if we are an image, a reflected image, are we really less than? No, we are not! You and I are a reflection.

The "You" Outside of "You"

Be afraid. Be very afraid. But I don't really have to tell you that. Most people are afraid of their true selves anyhow. We get a sensation of something more, but we back up from the uncharted territory of our greater selves.

Over "there" is scary. This is the domain of the gods! Keep the hell out! "I need you to be less so I can keep my "god" status", saith the Lord! Don't find out who you really are.

The truth is, all humans have an unlimited presence, and everything within the expanse of the presence of every individual is infinite. I call this, the "You" Outside of "You", and I can use a point of proof by pointing out the fact that we are made in God's image. If God is omnipresent, then we being made as an image must also be more than our physical presence; unlimited, and infinite within the structures that extend from us.

God never made anyone with a "period" at the end!

May I submit to you that our "messing up" is just our inability to handle the belief in what extends outside of ourselves. Our messing up is rooted in believing that we are less. Knowing the reflective characteristics of reality as it starts it's reflection from what can't be seen is paramount to understanding how to reflect your own unseen thoughts into reality.

But of course, there is a sense of inability that lurks here. This is because what you don't know does hurt you. Or better stated, what you decide not to know can and will hurt you. Let's look again at Eve and the fruit.

The Christian account of "the fall of man" states that Eve was told that if she partakes of the fruit, she would then "be like God". At this point, what Eve decided not to realize, is that being an "image" of who God is, meant she was already like God - an image. Therefore, she ate the fruit in the attempt to become who she already was. Isn't that the basis for all psychosis? It is the non-recognition of who you are, then the attempt to make up the difference at any cost?

To be or not to be is not the question. You are, is the answer.

Low evaluation of yourself will always be mirrored against your true status, thusly giving rise to the need to be better, and a good bit of this is done at a major cost and unnecessary sacrifice. First, there is no such thing as the "fall of man", it was only at this point that Adam and Eve became aware of the option of "less than" and then they built a relationship to "less than". Man did not fall in the beginning; man only refocused his attention and became exposed to another option. There is no such thing as "I can't", only you being focused on what can't be done, because what can be done is always there. You decide what you are exposed to by what you place your mind on and where you place your mind.

Eve chose to expose herself to an inability. Her status with God never changed, only her state. When something is not working for you in life, you are dealing with a state of being and not a status of being. It is never that you can't do something, because the "can" is always there. What are you tied into that gives you the sense of "can't"? When you change that, you will instantly change your state, which will then match your status.

Men don't fail; men only choose to see differently, and then live in what they only perceive to be a failure.

You are Complete

Man looks to feel complete. That's because his sense of completeness must be mirrored from a complete state, and that complete state is just as much of a reality than the physical. So, there is a need to experience substance and to gain a sense of completeness. You will find within the Genesis account in the Christian Bible, substance was fully provided for everyone, which is your Faith. Faith in what? Faith in who you are? Without knowing who you are, it is hard to feel substantive or have faith. This is why substance abuse is so prevalent. People are trying to get what they already have, go where they already are, and to be who they are already created to be by using off balanced relationships with people and substances to make up the difference. People are left feeling empty, along with the content of their souls being continuously drained.

The Spirit of the Mind Field

Without knowing who you are, it is difficult to have faith.

Every soul is full, but somehow we have learned to experience an empty state, not realizing that every individual is infinite and unlimited. It is the "You" that extends outside of "You". Everything in the Universe is completed and connected within you, which makes you a correct image of the Divine. Scientists are now discovering this fact more and more everyday as they research the human biological make-up and its psychological structures. Most of the foremost business leaders, great thinkers, and world trend-setters tap into this very fact every day and consistently retrieve into their lives "what's next".

Isn't this who God is? Isn't this the chief characteristic of The Universal. How is it that our minds do not pick up on this fact and we thusly live "less than" or live powerless lives?

Within this, these questions might come up... If our existence is so expansive and a reflection of the Divine, why don't we know everything? Why don't we have all the answers? Why can't I with one thought or one word make things right in my life or make things better? Since I can't do that, God must be" greater than" and I am "less than".

Well, let me ask you a few questions? If God is greater, why doesn't He just do all those things? He's God. Why doesn't He just say the one magic word and everything in your life pops right into place? Why does He just not feed all the starving people in the world and call it a day? Why doesn't He just give everybody some real money so there is no need to steal and embezzle? Why doesn't He just walk into every hospital and make everybody well? Hmmmmmm? It seems as though God's status at getting anything done runs a little parallel to ours.

At this point, this book might hit quite a few garbage cans. How dare you question God!!!?

Well, how dare you question yourself!!!?

How dare you deny who you are?

From this point on, the faint of heart should cease reading this book. I will employ a biblical text found in the second chapter of the

Book of Philippians, "Let this mind be in you, which was also in Christ Jesus, who thought it not robbery to be equal to God".

What???!!!?

Growth and Growing

We are asked here to have the same mind as God, along with the beginning thought, to be equal with Him. Is this a biblical stretch or what? The answer is no. The true seed of who you are lies in waking up to greater knowledge. Growth is staple to all existence, and experience is about moving from one existence to greater existences. More, and having more is central to all life, even the life of God.

Mankind does not have an "evil" problem, but a "sleeping" problem; asleep to what's "more".

Let's go back to the tough questions about our ability and God's ability to make things right. Notice whether you believe the biblical account of creation, the scientific account of the big bang theory along with evolution, or as a great number people currently do now, believe that evolution and creation are one and the same event. Despite your foundation, all of these stories begin with a small beginning, or as the Bible states, began with an earth that was without form and void. Either way, both grew throughout time to where we are now in Earth's history - into more. This fact is clear, that even God or the Universal Intelligence, whatever or whomever He is to you, He chose not to start with everything. The Universe and God Himself started with something small and unstable and grew it into more.

"More" is the purpose of life.

Here it is...

In the book of Genesis it says that the Earth was without form and void in the beginning. Look at where the Earth is now. Whatever state or condition you are in, you can always reach another state or a greater state. Even in the Bible, the Hebrew translation of "without form and void" is chaos. So where did chaos come from? Where did the "without form and void" come from? If the universe began as a small spec exploding into a massive existence, and then within billions of years evolved into what we see now, why start with a small spec? Where did the "small" come from?

Small is never a problem. Where you decide to grow from the "small" is what's important. Void is not an issue. How you decide to fill the void can be an issue. Chaos is not a problem, how you decide to grow over and above your chaos should be your focus.

Here is where we miss-define God. Here is where we dub the Universal Intelligence wrong. Here is where we make an erroneous description of the Spirit. Fullness is not about being complete, because fullness never really reaches a state of completion. The Universe is always in a state of growth and expansion. There is always more.

Fullness is about your ability to grow. Small, void, chaos, or things not being right, does exist, but it does not mean you are not without the ability to grow. You can grow from any point. That's the point of God, Spirit, or the Universal Intelligence – the ability to grow. You can grow from any point. It is your ability to grow that is the image of the Divine, not your size. So growth and growing is a responsibility.

From Small to Big, From Nothing to Something

One generally deals with psychosis by addressing the local issue of what's wrong in the moment versus spending time constructing in the non-local mind, which allows one to grow over and above undesired states. Everyone has a Mind Field that is infinite and is in a constant relationship to other Mind Fields that are also infinite. This Mind Field in biblical terms is stated as Spirit, and in the Genesis account of our earth's history, the Spirit hovered over the waters which was without form and void. So there are two presences that existed at one time. One is chaos (without form and void), and then the other is the Mind Field that exist over and above the chaos. The Mind Field was able to take that which was small and without form and void, and reshaped it and grew it. This Mind Field never dies or goes away.

So plainly stated, In the beginning God created the heavens and the earth and the earth was without form and void.

God, the Universal Intelligence started, with "without"!

So "without" can't be a bad place to start, because it is still who God is and it is a place where the Universal Intelligence Himself decided to start. The Universe began with a big bang, but before the "Big" bang there was "small".

So no matter what your state, you are still imaging who God is because of your Spirit within your Mind Field. From any given point, small or big, there is always the potential for growth and the potential for more. Psychology is about fixing or avoiding your current condition, but the "Mind Field" is about growing your current condition into something great. No matter where "small" is, the potential for growth is always in existence.

No one can ever say that their situation is limiting. Where there is a perceived limitation or chaos, there is always a mind. A Mind Field. Small is always the beginning to Big. Basically, small and big are the same thing, much in the same way as a seed being the same as the tree. All the components of the tree are contained in the seed, they are equal and one in the same. Even God chose not to start with everything, so even in our perceived smallness we are still like Him. Small does not mean separate or indifferent, it's just the beginning to big. The beginning to more.

The Non-Local "You"

Your Mind Field is non-local. You are non-local, fully present, but reflected into the local. You experience events locally, but "you" are non-local. When you hear music on the radio, the music doesn't occur locally within the radio. The music exists outside of the radio and then it is reproduced locally for your experience. Nine times out of ten, a band played the actual music years ago, but the music existed over time, and then through the expanse of FM waves or AM waves, the music is set to be received through your "local" radio. Just like the music actually exists outside of the radio, you exist outside of your local presence - this is the Mind Field. It is here where little work is ever done. A lot of times we fight to control our circumstances or resolve situations that are local, but all we need to do is to tune our radio channel to pick up what we desire in life.

No one can ever say that their situation is limiting, because both your Mind Field and your undesirable situation exist simultaneously, and both are a mirror image of the Universal Intelligence.

You have to have some guts to read the rest of this.

Yes. Everything mirrors God!

"Oohhh hell naaww! There is a devil, and he's bad, and he has all these demons screwing up my life! I can't get ahead because the devil, his demons, and his assigned people here on earth are after me to ruin my life and it's so hard! Even the bad that I do, the devil made me do it! Woe is me!"

What's In The Mirror?

God is "small to big". He is "chaos and Spirit", just as we are also "small to big". The Universe is "small to big", just as we are "small to big". Everything in the Universe is reflected from "small to big". A true picture of God is the state of Growth and Growing. We cannot define ourselves by our small existences or what might seem to be out of order, because that is never the finishing line, but always a starting point. "More" is always present because you have a mind or a Mind Field hovering over your chaos or your perceived limitations.

We can be excited about small or what's not working because it is still God. Spirit is always present. You are present. Count yourself in! So whatever your current circumstance is, it is always subject to grow. What you don't have is still a perfect picture. I'm going to help you to digest this as we go along.

Mind Field or Spirit hovered over the waters in the beginning, so the "waters" as stated here, represents the physical, which is your potential. Your potential never pops up into full existence at one time. Only your mind exists in fullness and has full presence, and is present. Your potential has to be shaped into something that you can enjoy, and your mind is capable of wonderful imaginations as to how things can be. You are always faced with the opportunity to create.

This is the Image of God. This is the mirror. Both what is not and what is. "What is not" is the Universe's specialty. So mirrored into you is "what is not" along with "what is", so you can always determine what will be. The problem is, is that a lot of times we chose to live in "what is not".

If God gave us everything at one time we would cease to be like Him. You and I have the same Spirit and Mind Field. Growing makes us just like Him. We are the Universe. We are His image. We are omnipresent, having full presence and being fully present, but we all start with what's small. Now we have to wake up to this fact. Not waking up, leaves you in the same conditions.

In the Christian Bible where the story was told about a crowd of 5000 plus people were being fed off of one boy's lunch; Jesus wasn't feeding the 5000, He was showing them how to take the little, multiply the little, and make it more.

You have what is small, and then you have the Mind Field.

You have what is without form, and then you have the Mind Field.

You have what is void, and then you have the Mind Field.

You have what is chaos, and then you have the Mind Field.

These things; chaos, without form, void, and smallness didn't come into existence as a result of the "fall of man", but they existed from the beginning as a part of who God is. Again, there was no fall, just an event where one's eyes were open to another part of reality – what is small. The only thing that came into existence that day is that Eve evaluated herself as being less than who she really was. This is the single most mitigating human problem, which is the source and the basis of anybody being stuck in life. What do you think of yourself?

Spirit is not just life; Spirit is also life to death and death to life. There is no point in existence where God does not exist. So we can get excited about what we don't have, because it is the stage of a Universal Creative Opportunity for Growth!

Removing Fear and Shame

You shouldn't be afraid of the little, or having less. The problem enters when you move to protect the little or to preserve the little that you have, or to keep it safe, and then by using your energy to keep from losing. Every seed must die to become a tree. The entire universe works this way. From small to big. From nothing to something. From messed up to something beautiful. Even from criminal to creator. Whether you made a mess out of your life, or whether you feel that you are at a disadvantage in life, it is a canvas for creation, a canvas to be something new and better tomorrow. This is all because you have an expansive Mind Field where nothing is an end.

This is who God, the Universal, the Supreme Being is - something new, something greater, but always extending from what was small, what was without form and void, and even full of chaos. This is where we image the Universal. We can take substance at any state and use our Mind Field to imagine something greater and then do it. The tree and the seed are exactly the same things. Time brings growth with a properly understood Mind Field.

The seed "messed up" and died, but after that it became an orchard.

Every baby, every seed, every business, every house, every venture, ducks, chimpanzees, alligators, space and time, is subject to the full picture of growth from small to big. Even sexually, the penis has to grow to perform a desired union. Why doesn't it just stay big! LOL!

Let's go back again to Adam and Eve. In the book of Genesis 3, God cursed the serpent that tempted Eve, and God also cursed the ground. Notice He never cursed Adam or Eve. It said that the Voice of God came to them walking in the garden, but the voice wasn't there to shame them, but yet Adam and Eve hid themselves from the Voice. It was within their own mind that they were ashamed. This caused them to be afraid of the Voice.

When you undervalue yourself, you are left exposed to what you think you are not. You then become afraid of your own image. Any shame leads to fear. You will notice that in the same chapter God said that Adam and Even became as one of Us. So where in this story is the "Fall" of man?

You have to properly evaluate yourself, even when things seem to be "not right". You might lose substance at times, but you will never lose yourself. So, stop hiding! Listen to the Voice that is consistently walking towards you, there to you to remind you that you are infinite. You are "more".

Fields of Substance

What is present before you is always great because it is still and will always be a part of who God is. Circumstances, good or bad, are always perfect for growth. But your focus should never be on the substantive existence, but on the Mind Field.

All I have is $1.00. That's good!

Things are not in place. That's good!

I have less than the next person. Still good!

All that is small as it concerns you, must grow by law!

I only have a small living space. Great!

I don't have a car. Even better!

I was abused when I was a child. Great!

I was molested when I was a teenager. Even better!

I'm not loved. How wonderful!

My parents never gave me any attention. Great!

People are so unfair to me. Great!

Nobody loves me. Great!

I am all alone. Even better!

Anything that is chaos is your starting point, because you have a mind. That mind is extensive, and your Mind Field is expansive!

I have HIV. Super!

I have a terminal disease. Awesome!

All of my money was lost. How powerful!

My car broke down. Great!

I am paralyzed. Great!

I was raised an orphan. Superb!

I'm getting kicked out of my house. Wonderful!

My mom died of cancer. Absolutely fabulous!

My boss treats me horribly! Outstanding!

Notice! Your mind is still there and is still alive. The fact that you can even complain about what's wrong, it shows that you have a mind that still works and can make assessments. Our minds can always call out a different story and reassess. Notice! No matter how horrible the situation is, the mind survives the impact enough to assess the situation. Now use that same mind to it to grow versus complaining. This is just the beginning of the true power of your Mind Field.

You can choose to live on the left hand within the substances of existence which will control you, or you can choose to live on the right hand where all substances are subject to the Mind Field and you gain control of your life and master your world!

I have been in jail for the past fifteen years. Great!

I'm a convicted felon. Greater!

I didn't graduate from high school. Super!

I'm on welfare. Absolutely marvelous!

I failed all my classes. Superb!

Your mind is still there!

I once was a thief. How exciting!

Nobody loves me. Sensational!

I have a disease. Good!

My business is failing. Outstanding!

These things make you more like God than you can ever imagine. He started there. Why doesn't God do all these great things to eliminate chaos? Well when you do them, then it is then done. This is our first peak into being just like Him. This is a peak into the "You" that exist beyond "You" into your own Mind Field.

Appendix

The 12 Points of Significance

If You Are Providing These and There is No Return,
it's not an Investment, Just a Loss!

1
(To Be Viewed)
The Investment of seeing and knowing a person.

To know a person as in their habits, favorite things, concerns etc.

To be concerned and having a person's back
based on what you see in them.

See, recognize, and care for one's issues.

Everyone needs someone to see and know who they are.

2
(To Be Comprehended)
The Investment of understanding a person.

Understanding of one's issues.

Willing to take in right information concerning a person.

Agreement and right action towards that understanding of the person.

Everyone has a need to be understood.

3
(To Be Engaged)
The Investment of active commitment.

Physical connection.

Partnership and unification.

Two way exchange or communication.

Everyone has a need to be touched in some way.

4
(To Be Praised)
The Investment of vocal affirmation of the good.

Recognition and hearing about good attributes.

Complimentary in nature towards a person.

Approvals of ideas, thoughts, visions…etc.

Everyone has a need to hear something good about themselves.

5
(To Be Believed)
The Investment of trust.

Take a position based on concerns verbalized, or character exuded.

Action oriented belief qualified by action oriented support.

Taking responsibility and acting on a person's
behalf based believing in them.

Everyone has a need to be trusted and believed in.

Appendix

6
(To Be Prioritized)
The Investment of making one special.

Acute attention in certain situations and areas.

Putting things aside in recognition of the other.

Allowing a person from time to time to be the most important.

Everyone has the need to feel number one sometimes.

7
(To Be Enriched)
The Investment of provision.

Bringing gifts or supplies not associated with earning.

Sharing your personal substance.

Making sure a person's needs are met.

Everyone has a need to receive.

8
(To Be Advanced)
The Investment of pushing one forward.

Progressing one's effort by means of time and efforts.

Providing leadership in your area of expertise to advance the cause of another.

To give an effort in setting a situation or circumstance right.

Everyone has a need to be mentored or pushed forward.

9
(To Be Rewarded)
The Investment of recognition.

To provide substance in recognition of what someone has invested in you.

Physical substance given in appreciation for efforts made.

Thank you and appreciation outside of verbal affirmation.

Everyone has a need to be appreciated in a tangible way.

10
(To Be Exalted)
The Investment of one's self into another.

Time spent in all areas of emotional investments.

Giving a sense of place based on your presence.

The gift of yourself that lift a person to another level, give status or empowers.

Everyone has a need to feel another's presence that builds their own presence.

11
(To Be Increased)
The Investment of addition.

To empower, enhance or enable in any way.

To see then add in a positive way time, effort, or substance.

To be an extension for someone where someone comes short.

Everyone has a need to be completed by the investment of another's effort and partnership.

12
(To Be Doubled)
The Investment of multiplication.

The experience of results.

Results that lead to more results.

Results that give a sense of place, home, completeness.

Everyone has a need to grow by the investment of another's effort or partnership.

    As you can see; your relationships and how they are set, play a vital role in your ability to see and experience your life in High Definition. This is the true beginning of everything economic. In order to live a fuller and more exiting life you must prepare yourself to receive your full supply of what's for you by setting your perception in line in order to focus on your own good.

Project 1

Relationship Forms:

Minor Authentications

Point	Person 1	Person 2	Person 3
Who Views You			
Who Comprehends You			
Who Engages You			
Who Praises You			
Who Believes in You			
Who Prioritizes You			
Who Enriches You			
Who Advances You			
Who Rewards You			
Who Exalts You			
Who Increases You			
Who Doubles You			

Major Authentications

Points of Focus	1	2	3
Books			
Classes & Courses			
Seminars			
Mentors			
Advisors			
Past Accomplishments			

Behavior Authentications

1. _____
2. _____
3. _____
4. _____

Name four practices that you will commit to that is geared towards what you want to accomplish.

Appendix

Determine your cycles in a chart that best fits your project:

	Viewed	Comprehended	Engaged	
Enriched				Praised
Advanced	Build	Build	Build	Believed
Rewarded	Energize	Energize	Energize	Prioritized
	Authenticate	Authenticate	Authenticate	
	Complete	Complete	Complete	
	Exalted	Doubled	Increased	

	Viewed	Comprehended	Engaged	
Enriched				Praised
Advanced				Believed
Rewarded				Prioritized
	Exalted	Doubled	Increased	

	Viewed	Comprehended	Engaged	
Enriched				Praised
Advanced				Believed
Rewarded				Prioritized
	Exalted	Doubled	Increased	

Project 2

Relationship Forms:

Minor Authentications

Point	Person 1	Person 2	Person 3
Who Views You			
Who Comprehends You			
Who Engages You			
Who Praises You			
Who Believes in You			
Who Prioritizes You			
Who Enriches You			
Who Advances You			
Who Rewards You			
Who Exalts You			
Who Increases You			
Who Doubles You			

Major Authentications

Points of Focus	1	2	3
Books			
Classes & Courses			
Seminars			
Mentors			
Advisors			
Past Accomplishments			

Behavior Authentications

1. _____
2. _____
3. _____
4. _____

Name four practices that you will commit to that is geared towards what you want to accomplish.

Appendix

Determine your cycles in a chart that best fits your project:

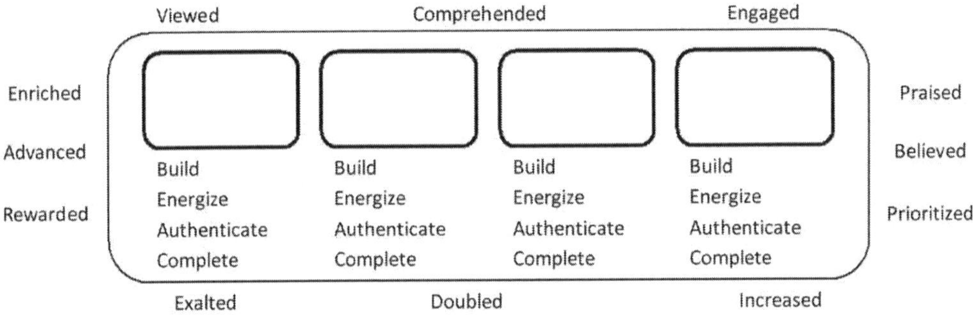

Viewed
Comprehended
Engaged
Enriched
Advanced
Rewarded
Praised
Believed
Prioritized
Build
Energize
Authenticate
Complete
Build
Energize
Authenticate
Complete
Build
Energize
Authenticate
Complete
Build
Energize
Authenticate
Complete
Exalted
Doubled
Increased

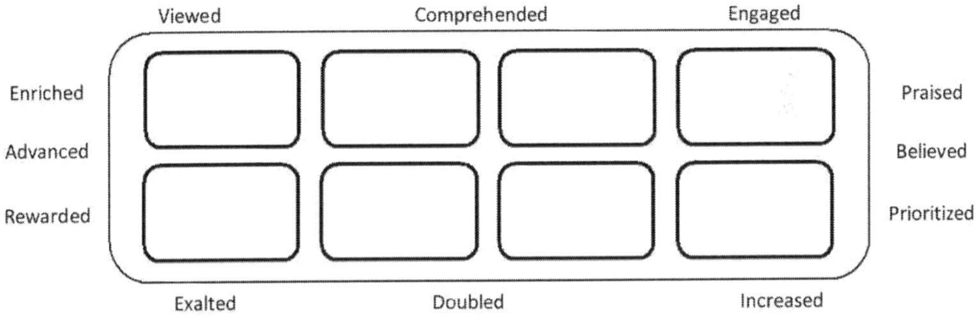

Viewed
Comprehended
Engaged
Enriched
Advanced
Rewarded
Praised
Believed
Prioritized
Exalted
Doubled
Increased

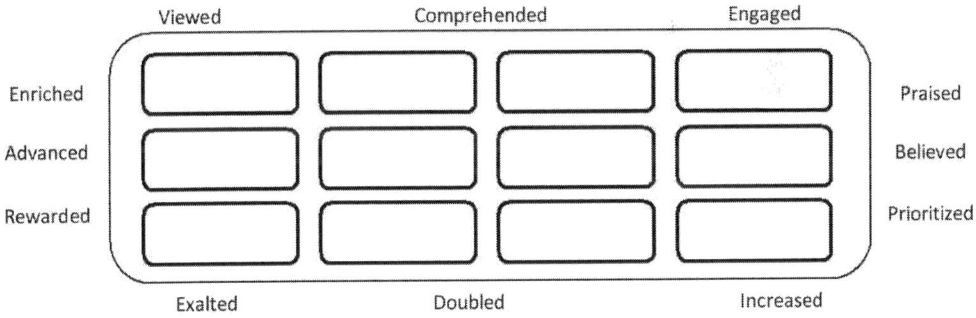

Viewed
Comprehended
Engaged
Enriched
Advanced
Rewarded
Praised
Believed
Prioritized
Exalted
Doubled
Increased

Project 3

Relationship Forms:

Minor Authentications

Point	Person 1	Person 2	Person 3
Who Views You			
Who Comprehends You			
Who Engages You			
Who Praises You			
Who Believes in You			
Who Prioritizes You			
Who Enriches You			
Who Advances You			
Who Rewards You			
Who Exalts You			
Who Increases You			
Who Doubles You			

Major Authentications

Points of Focus	1	2	3
Books			
Classes & Courses			
Seminars			
Mentors			
Advisors			
Past Accomplishments			

Behavior Authentications

1. _____
2. _____
3. _____
4. _____

Name four practices that you will commit to that is geared towards what you want to accomplish.

Appendix

Determine your cycles in a chart that best fits your project:

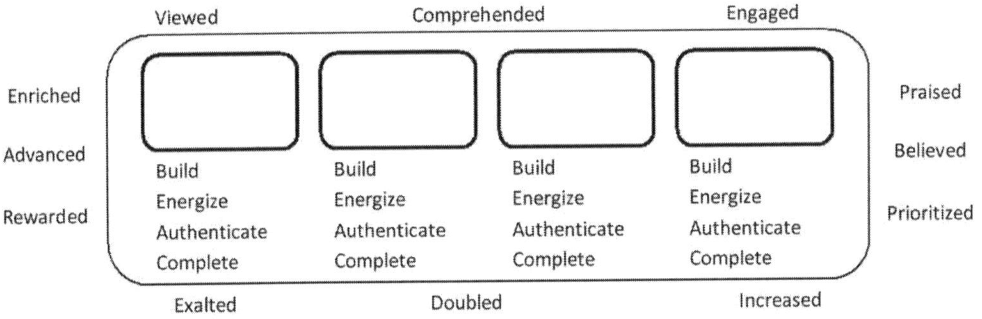

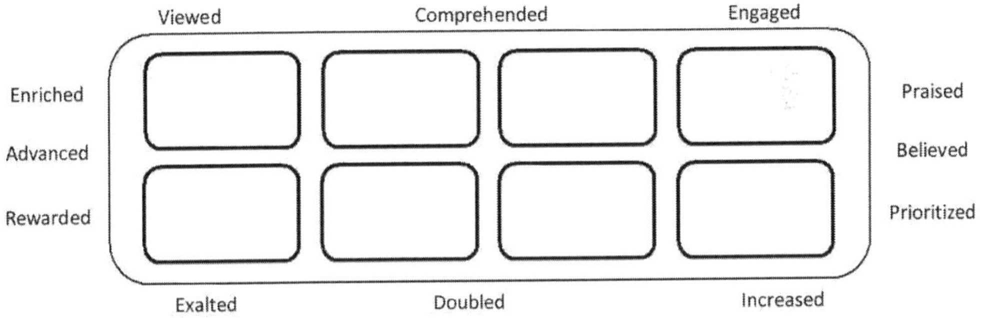

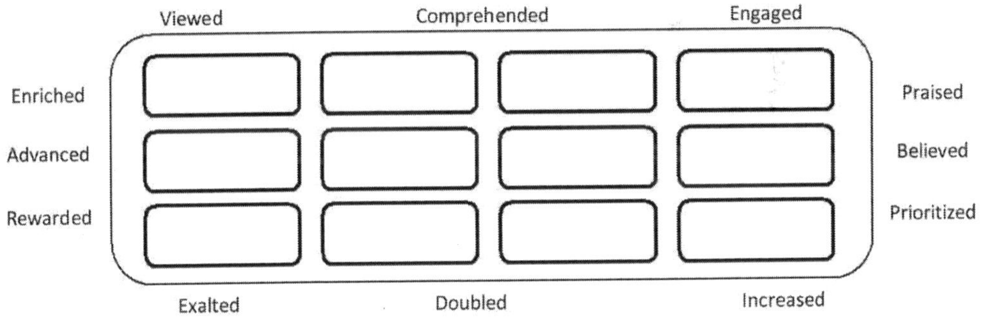

	Viewed	Comprehended	Engaged	
Enriched				Praised
Advanced	Build	Build	Build	Believed
Rewarded	Energize	Energize	Energize	Prioritized
	Authenticate	Authenticate	Authenticate	
	Complete	Complete	Complete	
	Exalted	Doubled	Increased	

(Chart 1: single row of four boxes with Build/Energize/Authenticate/Complete labels)

(Chart 2: two rows of four boxes each, with labels Viewed/Comprehended/Engaged across top; Enriched/Advanced/Rewarded on left; Praised/Believed/Prioritized on right; Exalted/Doubled/Increased across bottom)

(Chart 3: three rows of four boxes each, with same surrounding labels)

119

Project 4

Relationship Forms:

Minor Authentications

Point	Person 1	Person 2	Person 3
Who Views You			
Who Comprehends You			
Who Engages You			
Who Praises You			
Who Believes in You			
Who Prioritizes You			
Who Enriches You			
Who Advances You			
Who Rewards You			
Who Exalts You			
Who Increases You			
Who Doubles You			

Major Authentications

Points of Focus	1	2	3
Books			
Classes & Courses			
Seminars			
Mentors			
Advisors			
Past Accomplishments			

Behavior Authentications

1. _____
2. _____
3. _____
4. _____

Name four practices that you will commit to that is geared towards what you want to accomplish.

Appendix

Determine your cycles in a chart that best fits your project:

	Viewed	Comprehended		Engaged	
Enriched					Praised
Advanced	Build	Build	Build	Build	Believed
Rewarded	Energize Authenticate Complete	Energize Authenticate Complete	Energize Authenticate Complete	Energize Authenticate Complete	Prioritized
	Exalted	Doubled		Increased	

	Viewed	Comprehended		Engaged	
Enriched					Praised
Advanced					Believed
Rewarded					Prioritized
	Exalted	Doubled		Increased	

	Viewed	Comprehended		Engaged	
Enriched					Praised
Advanced					Believed
Rewarded					Prioritized
	Exalted	Doubled		Increased	

Made in the USA
Columbia, SC
06 March 2021